To: Nelson Yoder,

"Wilderness Chronicle"

I sincerely hope that you will enjoy at least a few passages in this little booklet. Feel free to use any part you wish in "Wilderness Chronicle"

Most Sincerely,

Jim MacConnell

JAMES D. MacCONNELL

DR. MAC, PLANNER for SCHOOLS

MEMOIRS OF MY FIRST 80 YEARS

JOHNSON/DOLE
Palo Alto, 1988

*Copyright © 1988 By
James D. MacConnell
All Rights Reserved*

Book typeset and paginated in Palatino 11/13 on a Compugraphic PowerView 10 and 8400 typesetter by Weekly Graphics, Palo Alto, California. Printed and bound by Braun-Brumfield, Inc., Ann Arbor, Michigan. Jacket design and book illustrations by Darla J.O. Van Bergen. Book design by José Corridor. Editorial Development by Carol Hegarty and the Executive Book Service, Palo Alto, California. Drawing of Dr. MacConnell on dust jacket, cover, title page and page 177 by William Turner.

Appreciation is extended to those who provided photographs and other factual information used in this book. Among them are Jean Niergarth Mott, Kathleen Niergarth Adams, Bessie Thomson Mellon, Ruth Ann Cochrane, Alma I. Nevin and Isabelle McConnell Walcutt.

*Library of Congress Catalog
Card Number 88-91184*

ISBN 0-929558-00-6

JOHNSON/DOLE
5 Palo Alto Square, Suite 1022
Palo Alto, California 94306

Table of Contents

	Part I	1908-1926
Long Rapids—The Early Years	1	
Long Rapids—The Later Years	18	
Our Family, the Roots of My Education	29	
The High School Years	42	
	Part II	1926-1943
Learn, Earn, Learn, Improve	57	
Professional Growth in Beaverton	71	
The Doctoral Program	93	
	Part III	1943-1948
A Race with the Draft Board	99	
Into the Navy	103	
Post War Adjustment	113	
Back in the Navy	117	
	Part IV	1948-1973
Down on "The Farm"—25 Years at Stanford	127	
Enter the Ford Foundation	135	
SPL Consulting at Stanford	145	
Private Consulting at Stanford	151	
	Part V	1973-1988
Beyond the Farm—Retirement Aftermath	162	
Beyond the Farm—Consulting Overseas	170	
	Part VI	In Conclusion
An Appreciation for My Friends	186	
Some Can Tell 'em; Some Can't	187	
Epilogue	193	

As the ARAMCO 747 Jet circled over the Saudi Arabian desert prior to landing at Dhahran, I looked out of the window and saw evidence of oil wealth beyond my greatest expectations. High rise buildings, oil derricks, huge pipes carrying desalinated water from the Persian Gulf and 6-lane highways abounded in a metropolis of a half-million people that two decades before had been sand and roving bands of nomads. "You've come a long way, baby," I reflected on the Saudis. And in the next moment thought, "And so have I."

Of course it took me longer: some seventy-odd years from Long Rapids, Michigan, population 60, where personal wealth was measured by success in scraping by from one potato harvest to the next; to a consulting contract with the Arabian American Oil Company (ARAMCO) to develop the educational specifications for a series of multi-million dollar elementary and secondary schools ARAMCO was to build for the Saudi Arabian government.

Of course there was a lot of time and experience in between Long Rapids and Dhahran and that is the topic of this book. Now on the eve of rounding out my first eighty years—half of them as a planner for schools—it seems appropriate to share some of those experiences with you.

So let's begin.

James D. MacConnell

Long Rapids—The Early Years

Most people have never heard of Long Rapids. In years of travel around the world I have yet to encounter anyone who knows where this village of some sixty people is located. My home town, or more correctly, my home village, is located in Alpena County, Michigan, about twenty miles west of Lake Huron and about halfway between the Equator and the North Pole.

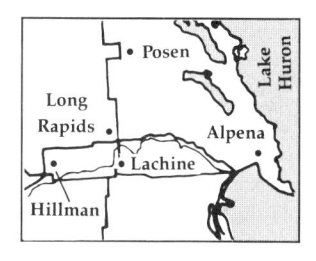

Named for the rapids of the Thunder Bay river that flows along its eastern border, Long Rapids had a population of only forty when I was a boy. It had two stores, a blacksmith shop, a butcher shop, a pool hall and a Saturday night ice cream parlor. It has never achieved the status of having a stop light. I can recall the installation of the first stop sign. The second one was put up years after I left.

Although I recall being slid down a Christmas tree by my Uncle Lewis McNeil before I could walk, my first real memory of myself as an individual is when I was about four years old. I was sitting on the steps of our rented house near Long Rapids, watching my parents walk across an adjacent field that was to be our farm.

I was born in that rented house on May 26, 1908, and I lived there until I was seven. It had originally been the property of my mother's parents, the McNeils, and on their deaths was the portion of the estate that went to my Uncle Jim. My mother had inherited an equivalent amount of money, a large portion of which she used as a down payment on our farm. I heard many discussions between my parents about the exorbitant price, $3,000.00, they paid for their eighty-acre farm.

"I Was Born"

My grandfather had built the house in which I was born at a cost of $2,000.00, a grand sum in those days, and it was one of the showplaces in the county. The front yard was surrounded by apple trees, and in the middle of the yard

Grandfather's House

1

The Party

was a rose arbor—the only rose arbor in my experience. In my imagination that rose arbor was the perfect setting for a big party, a party I planned innumerable times should the opportunity ever arise to give it. The clothing section of the Sears Roebuck catalog furnished me with sufficient pictorial information to know what the proper dress would be for the invited guests.

I saw a golden opportunity for the party when my mother and father were due to return home from a trip to Ann Arbor where they had been patients in the University Hospital. The elegant event was staged in the yard around the rose arbor—just as I had planned it so many times. No more glamorous affair has ever been held in Long Rapids. I must have had an extraordinary imagination, for I can clearly recall the guests arriving, mostly by horse and buggy, but a few in Model-T Fords. Their formal dresses and tuxedos were in full display.

I don't remember when my parents actually returned from Ann Arbor, and of course the formal party never really happened except in my mind, but the image is still vivid even today when I read about a special affair of that nature.

Mother with Grandfather and Grandmother McNeil and other kin in front of the house in which I was born sometime later.

WINTER HOLDS A COLD SPOT IN MY HEART...

So many of my childhood memories involve ice and snow that it is difficult now to accurately relate what a powerful influence winter had on life in Northern Michigan. Sitting on the steps of that rented house in late October, I thought about the dreaded winter that would be coming soon with its days and days of housebound isolation. The fall beauty of the red colors of the hard maples and the yellows of the soft maples was overshadowed even then by thoughts of the inescapable hardships of the winter to come.

Never having encountered hot weather in that far northern region surrounded by the Great Lakes, I was basing my judgment on very limited experience. Since then I have had many uncomfortable experiences with excessive heat and humidity. But even so, excessively low temperatures associated with acres of drifting snow have always held a special cold spot in my heart.

For Mother, Too

I know my mother disliked the cold as much as I did. She was a positive person, however, and always looked on the bright side of things. There were several instances where she and I together had extremely unpleasant experiences with cold weather and snow. Once when we were driving out of a side road in a cutter, Mother stopped the horse and got out to open the gate. This to the horse was apparently a signal to move on. Grabbing the reins as the horse went by, Mother was dragged several hundreds yards as the horse launched into a trot. Finally the horse halted. But I can still recall how frightened I was hanging on to the cutter, and how relieved I felt that Mother had withstood the ordeal, and that I had not been dumped in the snow.

Groundhog's Day

The next cold weather episode I remember was less dramatic but of a much longer duration. Groundhog's Day, February 2, brings a chuckle to some people. But as a child it was a serious event to me. I had heard that if the day were sunny and the groundhog saw his shadow, we were in for six more weeks of cold weather, and I knew that we had already had too much. As much as I enjoyed breaking off the icicles that hung from the edge of the roof, I always prayed for a cloudy Groundhog's Day. Even today I shiver when February 2 is mentioned. It was on that day in 1914 that my mother took me eighteen miles to Alpena in a cutter to have an operation for a growth under my chin. We left long before daylight with a charcoal heater at our feet and a supply of horsehide blankets over us. My father tucked us in and stressed the importance of keeping our faces covered as much as possible since the temperature was twenty degrees below zero.

The Surgery

The snow was deep, the sky was overcast, and the trip seemed to take forever. I doubt if it warmed up much all day. My only happy thought was that winter would soon be over, for the groundhog definitely did not see his shadow that day. Arriving in Alpena we left the horse at Mrs. Green's livery stable, where horses were kept during the day while people were shopping. Dr. McKnight's and Dr. McDaniel's offices were located on the second floor above a store. They removed the growth, and I can recall being supported by my mother as we came down the stairs afterwards.

The trip home seemed even longer. The charcoal heater was no longer warm, and I was in pain. I am mildly amused today when I hear someone talk about how quickly people are discharged from the hospital after surgery. On that Groundhog's Day seventy-odd years ago we had bypassed the hospital completely and exposed ourselves to eight hours of twenty-degree-below zero weather, and no one made anything of it.

And Father, As Well

My father had no fond feelings for the winter either. One icy February he donated his time, sleigh and team of horses to go to Alpena to pick up some used school desks for the new school in Long Rapids. The day he left was overcast. The air was strangely still and the smoke from the chimney did not go up as usual but hovered over the snow, staining it a brownish hue.

The Storm

That night a severe snow storm struck. It lasted two days and two nights and was followed by more below zero weather. Food was getting scarce at home and the wood we had stored was running out. (Customarily, we cut wood as needed from trees we had hauled from the long swamp some three miles away. In those days we could purchase all the standing timber we wanted from the state for one cent per cord.)

Finally, the evening of the fourth day, my father returned home riding one horse. He had successfully conquered the eight-foot snow drifts, but the desks, sled and other horse had had to be left behind in Alpena. The next week he had to make the trip again to complete his good deed.

I have watched the Winter Olympic Games on television. Much as I admire the contestants and vicariously share their successes and failures, the thought of having to endure the cold and snow in order to participate would discourage me even if I had the ability and opportunity to do so.

GOOD NEIGHBORS AND COLORFUL CHARACTERS

My father was always doing things for others, often beyond the call of duty. I remember his giving a neighbor's daughter two sheep, half our flock of four, when he felt that she needed them more than we did. Like him, our neighbors were for the most part, honest, hardworking, church-going citizens, similar to those in other small communities that formed the backbone of rural America in those days. Some of them, of course, were more colorful than others.

I had the pleasure of knowing a number of the early residents who were part of the folklore of Long Rapids — people like Sliver Stilwell, Bill Kelly, Charles Smith and Mrs. Bodi.

Sliver Stilwell

Sliver Stilwell, before my time, had driven the stage coach from Hillman to Alpena, a distance of some forty miles. His regular stop was at Long Rapids, the halfway point, where he fed and rested his horses. His team was made up of one large horse and one small one, the larger one usually leading the way by half a body length. When my father mentioned that the large horse was much faster than the little one, Sliver responded, "Not too much faster. We've come all the way from Hillman, and that's all he's gained so far."

Bill Kelly

Bill Kelly lived on a little farm a mile or so north of Long Rapids near the sunken hole region. Bill had never learned to read or write, or even tell time, although he always carried a huge pocket watch attached by a heavy gold chain. Small groups liked to gather around and ask Bill what time it was by his gold watch. Bill would pull the watch out of his pocket and hold it in his hand so that each onlooker had an opportunity to see its face. At that point he would put it back in his pocket and always make the statement, "Who in Hell would think it was that late?"

The Reader

Since Bill was somewhat ashamed that he had never learned to read, he tried to cover up the fact in various ways. When anyone would visit him, for example, he would pick up a newspaper and comment on the largest picture. But the day came when one of his neighbors came into the living room and took Bill by surprise. Bill hurriedly reached to pick up the paper off the floor, but in his haste held it upside down. As he stared at the picture, he said, "Holy Christ, a big wreck on the ocean—ship upside down!"

The sunken hole area near the Kelly farm was a region where, over the ages, water had eroded limestone into a series of underground caverns.

In some places the roofs of the caverns had collapsed, leaving huge holes that were hundreds of feet across and varied in depth. In the spring, water would pour down and disappear. A story that was never proven was one about the pipe-smoking farmer driving by with a load of baled hay who was dumped into a sunken hole along the highway when his load shifted. Supposedly he came up in Thunder Bay some fifteen miles away with his pipe still lit.

Mr. Smith

Another old-timer, Mr. Smith, spent a good deal of time hanging around Niergarth's store. Feeling that he knew Mrs. Niergarth well enough to call her by her first name, which was Nina, he proceeded to do so. Mrs. Niergarth took exception and promptly informed him that her name was Mrs. Niergarth and that he was to address her that way. Taken aback, Mr. Smith sputtered, "OK, Nina. I will, and from now on Nina, I will call you Mrs. Niergarth, by God, I will, Nina."

Mrs. Bodi

Mrs. Bodi lived up on the Long Swamp, a heavily wooded area some one hundred miles long and fifteen miles wide. She lived with Saul Stone, although she was not married to him. As Mrs. Bodi would drive by our home, on her rounds to collect rags to make rugs, my mother would invariably say,"There goes Mrs. Bodi. You know she lives with Saul Stone, but they aren't married." Today Mrs. Bodi would not be such a rarity.

Harry Wise

Another person who was kind when I was growing up was Harry Wise, the RFD mailman. He had an automobile and once a year would let me ride with him over his entire route. We talked about lots of different things and he was always encouraging when I told him about my dreams and aspirations. He and his wife Cynthia Monroe later donated a recreation addition to the Long Rapids Church.

ETHNIC MOSAIC

Long Rapids was populated primarily with families of Scottish descent. In fact, if one were to eliminate the MacArthurs, McMillans, McLarens, McConnells, Lumsdens and Thomsons, there wouldn't be many people left.

The region north of the sunken holes, however, was settled for the most part by people whose ancestors came from Norway. Their community, which included a store, post office and a few houses, was known as Leer. North of Leer most of the people were Polish, and Posen was their trading center. North of that area and on to the Straits of Mackinac, the land had been settled by German families. In my youth, the lines of distinction between the ethnic groups were marked, but not so today.

There are thousands of rural farming communities of this nature that don't make the daily news or the history books. In them youth are brought into the world but have little opportunity to stay on the small farms because the small units become parts of the larger units and disappear. Youth must leave to seek more rewarding opportunities or remain and be satisfied with a marginal existence.
Being the oldest boy in our family, I was early oriented to the fact that probably I would not live my total life in Long Rapids.

Our neighbors to the near north, the Norwegians, were excellent citizens, farmers and church-goers who scarcely ever got into trouble. Learning to speak English was usually difficult for the early settlers, and the following story was probably created to poke a little fun at the Norwegians' language problems.

Supposedly a robbery had been reported and two sheriff's officers had received word that the robbers were hiding in the Leer general store. Indeed, the robbers had taken refuge in a couple of empty grain bags in the back room among many bags that were filled with sleigh bells. As the officers walked by the bags, they kicked each one and heard a slight jingle. When they kicked the bag in which one of the thieves had hidden, however, the sound that emerged was, "Yingle, yingle, yingle."

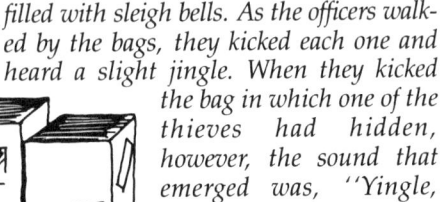

BEGINNING GRADE SCHOOL

It was early September, 1914, when I started to school. This was before kindergartens were organized in our county, which accounted for my not starting before I was six.

I looked forward to the first morning as my first venture away from home without an adult accompanying me. To my great disappointment Mrs. Ruben Thomson, who lived a half-mile west of us, accompanied Nelson, who was a year older than I, to our place. Then I learned that both of our mothers were going to accompany us to school on our first day. I protested vigorously, took Nelson by the sleeve, and the two of us started off to school with our lunch boxes and first grade readers in hand.

The Jones School

The Jones one-room school, which was located about a mile from home, served as the center of learning for the community. The grade organization was first through eighth with each class averaging around five or six members. There were fewer seventh and eighth graders and they were envied by the rest of the student body. Few, if any, of the pupils had parents who had attended high school. Some of the teachers had attended high school, but I can't recall having a teacher in that school who had attended as much as a year of college. I well remember having had three teachers in one year each of whom had no more than eight grades of formal schooling.

For years the school met none of the requirements for what was then known as a standard school—indoor toilets, a bubbler drinking fountain, single student seats attached to the floor, windows so located as to bring light only over the left shoulder and a circulating hot air furnace. Someone did inaugurate a hot soup program, which meant that the soup could be heated on top of the stove and distributed to those who hadn't forgotten to bring cups.

I liked all of the pupils, although at times I was envious of the Behling children for they were of the Lutheran faith and would dress up on Good Friday morning, sit on the swing chair on their porch, and wave to us as we trudged by to school. I begged my parents to let me join the Lutheran Church, but my pleas fell on deaf ears.

Roughing It

In the center of the room was a cast-iron wood stove that had no fan device to distribute the heat. The lucky pupils were those who sat on the inside row closest to the stove. Those of us who drew the desks near the windows would use the blocks prepared for firewood as stools until the time came to burn up our seats. The glass panes for a number of windows had been replaced with cardboard, but it wasn't very satisfactory. The cardboard helped keep out the cold but also shut out the light. I personally favored being a few degrees warmer. One's eyes could adjust to semi-darkness, but turning the pages of a textbook while wearing mittens was cumbersome. On one occasion it was so cold outside that my father came with a team of horses and a sled to take us home. It was nearly as cold inside the school.

The Textbooks

A school library was nonexistent so most of us brought a personal book for the subjects requiring textbooks. I remember little about the contents of any of my books, but with the help of the teacher, my sister and parents, I did learn to read. I do recall a picture of Thor, the Thunder god, driving his horses over a cloud with lightning flashing around him that impressed me no end. I also remember a geography book that added to my discontent as I read about places where supposedly there was no snow in the wintertime.

Jones School circa 1914. Little Jimmy front row far left; sister Isabelle front row fourth from right.

A poem about the sandpiper also was intriguing to me. The first stanza went like this:

> Up and down the beach we flit
> One little sandpiper and I.
> Gathering driftwood bit by bit
> As the scudding clouds pass by.

I asked the teacher what a sandpiper was. She didn't have the slightest idea. One boy said that it was like a groundhog, and it dragged wood. Not having access to a dictionary, it was not until I got into high school that I found out what a sandpiper was.

And Recess

Recess held no fond memories for me. I remember playing "Duck On The Rock" and another game in which a rock was placed on one end of a long plank laid over a large log serving as a fulcrum. The game was to place a large stone at one end while hitting the other end with the blunt end of the woodshed axe. The result was that the stone was hurled several hundred feet. So much for recess.

Motivation

Although the school was by and large dull and unimpressive both inside and out, I vividly remember the plaque located over the blackboard in the front of the room. The plaque had a picture of an old gnarled hand on it with a motto printed in bold type, "I WILL DO MY BEST." The motto bothered me, for I felt that there were times when I was letting it down.

The hand pictured on the plaque was that of Mr. Little, our County School Superintendent. Every year he was obligated to visit each rural school in the county. We were well coached by the teachers to stand and hold up our right hand while the teacher welcomed him into the school. Then we would repeat after him as he stood there with his right hand raised, "I will do my best."

There was one advantage in attending the Jones School. I always knew what subject matter was being covered in all eight grades. In retrospect I can recall few specifics that I actually learned in grade school except the multiplication tables. I learned them so well, in fact, that it caused me trouble. For years I found it difficult to segregate any one figure that I needed without beginning at the top of the "times" table.

MOVING NEARER TOWN

By 1915 we were living in our new house, and it was a half-mile closer to Long Rapids. My folks had chosen the plan from that of a house they saw in Rogers City, on Lake Huron some twenty-five miles away. It was one of the nicer houses in the community and had a full basement. This was my first encounter with close neighbors. The Butlers lived across the road from us in a little white house. They were a novelty to me. They had already reared their family, which meant that they were older than my parents. Also, they were Catholics. I was rather amazed to find that Mrs. Butler's pies tasted like Protestant pies, and this discovery verified my mother's statements that they were real nice people.

The New House

We had a few sheep, and Mrs. Butler knitted socks and sweaters for me. She carded the raw wool and spun it with her own spinning wheel. The sweaters were bulky and quite heavy, but warm, and the socks were hard and oily. I used to tell my father that the sheep followed me around because they thought I was one of them. I looked forward to the time when I could buy things that were made by machinery and were not so smelly and bulky.

Niergarth's Store

At an early age I became aware that not only did I not have money to spend but neither did my folks. That fact preyed on my mind even then for I knew that they had many more needs than I had that could not be satisfied.

12

To this day I dislike the words, "Charge it," because of the times my mother sent me to Niergarth's store with a grocery list. When Mrs. Niergarth would tell me how much I owed, I had to say, "Charge it," because our family was always so short of cash. I'll never forget the look on Mrs. Niergarth's face as I took the groceries out of the store. Wistfully, I always compared our family to the Behling's, who not only had cash to spend, but also had a steel safe in their house. I constantly begged my father to buy a safe so we too would have money.

The other store in Long Rapids was Marsten's. Mrs. Marsten made bread, which she baked in her own oven since their house was connected to the store. The bread was sold out of a barrel and when the barrel was opened it smelled like today's modern bake shop. Mrs. Marsten's bread was full of holes, which differed from my mother's bread, which was firm. My father used to say that when we bought a ten-cent loaf of bread from Marsten's, five cents went for air and the other five for bread.

The first Christmas presents my sister and I ever bought for our parents were purchased from Marsten's store. My gift to my father was a pair of arm bands that men wore to keep their shirt sleeves from coming so far down on their wrists. I don't recall what my sister's gift to our mother was, but no doubt it too was something in the ten-cent range.

Marsten's also sold little iron horses on pedestals that were used to decorate the clocks that usually were located in the living or dining room of each home. At that time, there was nothing in the world I wanted more than one of those horses. When in the store I always made it a point to spend a minute or two admiring them so tantalizingly displayed on a high shelf. Then one night the store burned and so did the horses. I remember thinking that if Mr. Marsten had only given me one of those horses, at least one of them would have been saved.

Marsten's

For years we had a wide ironing board that came from the Marsten home. It was fascinating to me because, at one time, when Mr. Marsten was taken suddenly ill with appendicitis and couldn't be moved, a doctor from Alpena came and operated on him while he lay on the ironing board.

Perhaps because our lives were so simple and hardworking, certain events in town stand out as especially memorable. One of them was the annual Long Rapids Fair.

The Annual Fair

In spite of an average ninety-day growing season in that part of Michigan, a remarkable number of fruits and vegetables weathered the early frosts, and the best were proudly exhibited on long tables at the Fair. Jellies, jams, pies and cakes were on display as well as handiwork of all kinds including quilts made by the local Ladies' Aid and other groups from outlying churches. I always wondered why the judges, who usually came from Alpena, were capable of awarding the prizes, while the farmers and their wives who raised the products or did the needlework were never accorded the honor of being named judges. Pulling contests for horses were the chief competitive activities that attracted the men's attention. George Monroe always won with a team in harnesses laden with highly polished brass.

There were a number of foot races for the youngsters. Cash prizes were given, and I always looked on with envy, for I was not athletically inclined. I am certain passing even one contestant in a race would have helped my morale.

July the Fourth

The Fourth of July was another big day in Long Rapids. Everybody talked about going to the town celebration. I watched people celebrate, but the only ones who seemed to act differently than they did when I saw them in their homes were the limited number who had partaken of too much liquor. Some of them were apparently having a good time, but others were fighting. The glamor of the whole affair escaped me since the fire-crackers, ice cream and candy all cost money, and I had none to spend.

The one great thing about the Fourth of July for me was that we would milk the cows late in the morning and then not milk them at night. In looking back, I imagine the cows didn't look forward to the Fourth as much as I did.

The Town Hall

The first town hall was a two-story structure that housed most of the community gatherings. It was not a large building, but my father said that it was built for just $1.25 per square foot. All the lumber had come from local timber tracts, and no doubt a considerable amount of donated labor helped to keep the cost down as well.

Cost for such a building today wuld vary from $100.00 to $200.00 per square foot but would include more of the luxuries to which we have become accustomed.

I don't remember what happened to the old town hall but the new one that took its place is now located on the south side of the village on the north bank of Thunder Bay River a mile or so above the rapids. I worked half a day shoveling gravel into a concrete mixer to help pour the foundation of the new town hall. That evening I was convinced that if further education would free me from work of that nature, I had better stick to my books. Today the town hall hosts all township activities, including elections, dances and dinners. It draws from the city of Alpena, some eighteen miles to the east, and the village of Hillman, an equal distance to the west.

The Church

My early disenchantment with the cold weather was reinforced later in my youth when I became the Sunday morning janitor of our local Congregational Church—a job that guaranteed my steady attendance. I remember that worshippers sat nearly freezing in the cold church, listening to the unconvincing pastor threaten them with the intense heat that would welcome them after death should they stray from the narrow path and give in to sin.

As I sat in the back row, in the closest seat to the wood-fired furnace in the basement below, I knew in my heart that a little sin accompanied by a moderate amount of heat would lure me along the Christian route with more enthusiasm.

Its Influence

But even though the sermons left something to be desired, the church was very important to all of us. In most small communities the church plays a role as a catalyst, and the smaller the community, the greater the church's influence. The Long Rapids church was no exception. Community gatherings centered around the church. In addition to regular church and Sunday school activities, the weddings, funerals and Christmas programs always drew practically everyone in the community. Kitchen facilities made it possible for the Ladies' Aid Society to sponsor fund-raising suppers to supplement the Sunday collections. Our church started out as Congregational but for a number of years it was non-denominational as membership in outlying places of worship decreased and better roads made it possible for people to get to a centralized church in a trading center.

Our Church, 1912

At about five years of age I walked up the aisle of the church, faced the congregation, and said "Look at my new suit." This may have been my first appreciation of clothing—one I've had all my life.

16

The outside stairway was always a bone of contention of my mother, who objected to the steps that were almost impossible to use, expecially for funerals when covered with ice in the winter. June and I later made it possible to extend the length of the church and move the stairs inside. I wish that my mother could have had the satisfaction of seeing and attending activities in this rehabilitated facility.

Our Church, 1982

From time to time religious cults sprang up, but they were generally short-lived. My father used to tell about one group founded north of our village that required baptizing through the ice as a cleansing process for salvation. The demise of that group occurred following a ceremony when a 250-pound man was wrapped in a blanket, and lowered through a hole in the ice. When a swift river current quickly pulled him downstream, the minister is said to have turned to the group and stated, "The Lord giveth and the Lord taketh away. Bring on another sinner!"

People forget your pleasant thoughts and deeds, but remember your complaints as is demonstrated by the story about the Mother Superior who was visiting a convent and requested an evaluation from each nun. All were complimentary except one little nun who said, "The food here is lousy." Ten years later the Mother Superior made a return visit and those in attendance made similar complimentary comments as before except the same little nun who responded, "The mattresses are lumpy." The Mother Superior's reaction this time was, "Gripe, gripe, gripe, Sister. All you do is gripe!"

Long Rapids—The Later Years

Snow was my ever-present enemy five months per year. It was usually accompanied by cold weather, and the amount of snow on the ground determined what you could and could not do during those short days and long nights. Snowdrifts prevented seeing the barn from the house and it was necessary to climb over those drifts a dozen times a day to care for the needs of the farm animals.

It is difficult now to become enthusiastic about a story that is built around cattle and snow. I knew, though, that previous generations had had it worse. My folks often referred to our good fortune in living during a time when kerosene was available less than a mile away. My grandfather had had to walk eighteen miles to Alpena to buy kerosene if he wanted to have a much brighter light that that provided by candles.

Buying kerosene by the gallon, carrying it home, cleaning soot from lamp chimneys with crinkled up newspaper, trimming lamp wicks to prevent excessive collection of soot, and filling the lamp were all distasteful jobs, for they were always accompanied by the smell of kerosene. The only enjoyable part of the process was pulling the gumdrop stopper from the spout of the kerosene can, and eating it. Since then, oddly enough, gumdrops don't taste the same; I must miss the kerosene flavor!

THE SEASONS

Today, it is common to hear people extol the virtues of changing seasons. But I assure you that those virtues were lacking in the early nineteen hundreds in Long Rapids when the lack of transportation and inadequate communication trapped people for five cold, wintery months a year. The other three seasons were crammed into seven months. Spring was great except that it was too often invaded by a late winter holdover. Autumn was a short picturesque experience that would soon be devastated by Winter. An early frost was often the culprit that cut down the few rewards of a farmer's hard working summer. I learned early in life that a maximum ninety-day growing season was much too short to guarantee a mature crop. I also became aware that an eighty-acre farm in Alpena County, with at least twenty-five percent of the land unusable, was not capable of producing enough to provide a family's food and still have much of anything left to sell.

Farms are traditionally thought of as good places to rear children. As I look back on my youth on the farm I have mixed emotions about the validity of that thought. I feel that its truth depends upon the farm location, size and productivity.

BOYHOOD ADVENTURES

Like most young boys, attending school was not exactly my favorite pastime, so I was quick to take advantage of other opportunities that arose. In early fall the arrival of the threshing machine to thresh the few bushels of grain that we had grown was one of those occasions. Threshing presented a difficult time for my mother who had to prepare a mid-day meal and at times supper for some twenty to twenty-five men. Even though one of the neighbor women usually would come to help, it was a major chore. When the men lined up to wash prior to eating, they made quite a commotion as they congregated around the low table that was covered with wash bowls.

The Young Thresher

One morning before school I was allowed to climb up on the threshing machine platform and, assuming the operational position, to guide the long pipe from which the straw and chaff came out of the machine onto a gradually increasing stack on the ground.

When it was time to go to school, I felt a tug on my pant leg and from the corner of my eye saw my mother. I stood rigid and pulled the lines that steered the spewing straw pipe into neat piles. At the same time, I saw my father wave her off, and as she departed for the house, I knew I had become master of the straw department for the day. Later, I even washed my face in one of the metal wash bowls and ate with the threshers at noon.

The Great Disker

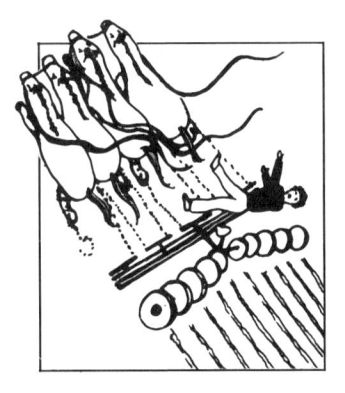

Disaster!

The next opportunity to leave school for the greater part of an afternoon came a few weeks later. At breakfast time, my father mentioned having to go to a farm credit meeting which meant that he could not finish disking a twenty-acre plot that was on his schedule for the day. Although I was only nine years old, I quickly volunteered to take over and finish the job.

Father turned over the reins and gave me my first opportunity to drive a four-horse-abreast team, pulling a twelve-foot-wide disk harrow. Had the day been routine, I would have had it made, but within an hour or so, one of the chain tugs came loose and wound around a back leg of one of the horses. Dan was a rangy sorrel who was much more excitable that the other three horses. With one lunge he took the lead, and all four horses headed toward the thirty-foot-wide lane that led to the barn. I was immediately catapulted off the seat and fortunately landed behind the disk. Since Dan had more speed than the others, he steered them into the fence before they reached the lane.

I shall never forget the tangled mess that met my eyes as I finally caught up to the pileup of horses, fence and harnesses and heard the terrifying noises coming from the horses as they lay on top of, underneath and beside each other. I used my new pocket knife to free the horses without major damage to them or the harnesses and was amazed to see how much a horse's head could be twisted and pulled without its being killed.

When my father returned home, I was happily surprised at his sympathetic understanding of the tragedy. He demonstrated great concern about any injuries that I might have incurred, and expressed relief that I was breathing and in one piece rather that in the six-inch sections that would have been left of me had I fallen in front of the disk.

I guess my childhood was quite normal. The trips to Alpena on the gravel roads with my father in a wagon loaded with apples was both jarring and boring. We always took the river road and once the two towers of the St. Francis

Catholic Church came into view, I knew that in another hour we would be in Alpena selling apples on the street. The trip one way took about four hours and fifteen minutes; the same length of time that it now takes the Concorde to fly from London to Washington, D.C. The apples did not enhance our cash flow too much. Nor did the long ride enhance their beauty although it did quicken their preparation for cider. I always objected to having storekeepers make me an offer for apples and yet always have a fixed price on things they sold to me.

FIRST EARNING EXPERIENCES

The payment of allowances to children by parents receiving regular income has always been fairly common. For farm children in my community it was not the rule. A source of spending money was hiring out to neighboring farmers to help with the harvest. This was good for at least five dollars. However, if the work was in exchange for work the neighbors had done on your parents' farm, payment was skipped and the labor yielded naught as far as the children were concerned.

The Bill Collector

Being potato producing country, Northern Michigan lent itself to job opportunities picking up potatoes behind the digging machine. One neighbor informed me, after I had worked a day picking up potatoes, that he would pay me later. This was not one of my better trips home, but it alerted me to the need for a payment arrangement prior to rendering service. The debt in this case lingered on, and every day I thought of more reasons why I should be paid. Winter came and still no pay. Then one day I saw the neighbor coming down the road with his team of horses and sled. The road was confined to one lane because of ten-foot snowbanks on each side, and I saw my opportunity to close in on my debtor. I stood in the middle of the road and gave him no choice except to run over me or to stop. He chose the latter and requested an explanation for my behavior. "I want the fifty cents you owe me." He reached into his pocket and presented me with the shiniest fifty-cent piece I had ever seen. It was with great satisfaction that I notified the family that night that I had collected.

The Banker Another day when I was picking up potatoes near the road, I saw the local banker drive by. I knew that he resided in Lachine, another village of about seventy-five people, located south of us. He was well-dressed and was driving a Rickenbacker automobile. As we breathed in the cloud of dust he left behind, I asked my father how the banker had been able to get so much money. I was told that he had gone to college and saved his money by putting it in a bank. To me, this was one more reason for going to college, plus a reinforced incentive to put money in the bank. Soon thereafter I deposited thirteen dollars, my total savings, in the Lachine Bank. Carrying the bank book around to show the others in school was a matter of great pride. I was, however, somewhat disappointed with the small amount of earnings I was realizing from the four percent interest.

Bank Failure Within months of my deposit rumors were making the rounds that the bank was in trouble and that there was a good possiblitiy that all funds deposited in it would be lost. My father went to the bank and witnessed the "Closed" sign being posted on the door. His statement when he came home was that he had heard of banks going "bust," but he never thought he would ever see one busting in his face.

We had a meeting that night. The discussion centered around the fact that things can happen that are not anticipated.

Shortly after the bank closed, the banker stopped by to see my father. I rushed in the house and asked mother for a screwdriver so I could take at least thirteen dollars' worth of things off the Rickenbacker. She and I had a serious discussion about more ethical ways to get even, so I faced reality and lived in hope that some day I would recover at least part of my capital investment.

Just prior to my entering high school some years later, I received a check for three cents from the receiver of the bank. No one can ever convince me that things that happen to youth are not lasting. I have never had a savings account in a bank since that day. I hear from others that savings funds are now insured, but I have never had the nerve to find out for sure.

WORLD WAR I

World War I was much different from the wars that followed as far as I am concerned. I remember lots of enthusiasm and music—everyone seemed to want to be part of it. "Over There," "Johnny Get Your Gun" and many other songs of that nature were being sung at all social gatherings. I recall standing on a stool to participate in the singing with the local young men, many of whom were already in uniform. My only regret then was that I hadn't been born some ten years earlier so I could also enlist.

As the war got into full swing, "Help save the world for democracy" was on everyone's lips. I didn't know what it meant, but I soon learned that being a second generation German was not an enviable position to be in. Even at my young age I knew that the stories being circulated about our German neighbors, the Behlings, were not true. They were one of the few families that had money in our community. I knew how hard they had worked for it, and could not imagine their sending a large share of it to Germany to "Support the Motherland" as the rumor had it.

This early observation convinced me that people become irrational when outside pressures change their normal life patterns. Since then I have been careful to closely scrutinize newspaper articles, especially headlines, and radio and television news broadcasts that are presented on a flash basis oftentimes more for effect than for fact.

Involvement

I also learned that the psychology of arousing people to become aware of a crisis necessitates using media devices that will result in total involvement of all age groups. Knitting wash cloths for the soldiers was probably not the best use of my skills and time, since mine resembled diapers more than wash cloths, but doing so made me aware that there was a war on and that I was helping.

Thrift Stamps

Although I feared that my father would be required to serve in the military, I enjoyed the fact that I got Wednesday afternoons off from school to sell thrift stamps. They sold for 25 cents and twenty of them could be turned in for a five-dollar War Savings Bond. Calling on the residents of Long Rapids and the surrounding farm area made me realize that there were people who had less than we had, as well as others who had prospered more. One family revealed the fact that they had saved three thousand dollars. At times people would give me as much as a twenty-five cent piece to keep because of the war effort I was exhibiting by my enthusiastic salesmanship.

While I found the thrift stamp experience a highlight, the reality of the war became clearer to me when the pictures and the headlines in the "Alpena News" reported the army casualties in France and at sea, where German U-boats were sinking our ships.

As time went on, the return of the wounded soldiers was yet another reminder that war was not all fun and games. The services for the casualties in the flag-draped caskets at the front of the church were unpleasant for me and I always tried to find some other task to perform when my parents attended those sad functions.

THE FLU EPIDEMIC

1918 was a time of sadness for me. World War I was still underway and so was the epidemic of Spanish Influenza. The disease had spread from Europe and there was no cure. People who were exposed to someone who had it usually became very ill with a high fever and many died. This was particularly true of children. One of our neighbors lost three children in one night.

Watching rough boxes being taken to the cemetery and placed by grave sites yet to be dug was depressing.

I feel that we had average medical attention. Our physician, Dr. Purdy, was blind, but in spite of that he was probably as competent in dealing with this new disease as most doctors were at that time. If his services were needed, we would hang a lighted lantern on the mailbox. The doctor with his driver in a horse and cutter would stop, make his house call, and leave appropriate medicine for those in need. One of my jobs was to keep oil in the lantern.

Upon occasions when my desire for money became too obvious, my parents would bring me back to reality. As the Spanish Influenza was taking its toll, one of our neighbor's little girls passed away. The grandfather came to our house and asked my father if I could be one of the pallbearers. I agreed to do so when Father explained in detail to me what the duties would be. The month was February, the temperature was below zero, and the snow was blowing in a high wind. After the casket was lowered into the ground and my parents and the mourners had left the gravesite, I remained. My response to my father's request that I come with him was, "I haven't been paid yet." That statement initiated another meeting at home where the theme centered around the fact that much is done during a lifetime where no compensation is realized or even expected.

Death was becoming a frequent reality as more and more people became exposed to the flu and doctors were unable to help. Observing grave diggers, usually neighbors, chopping out frozen soil to accommodate the rough boxes as the snow swirled around the tombstones was depressing to me. I was fortunate in that I did not contract the disease, but my mother was a victim, and she had many bad days and nights. She probably would not have survived had she not had a strong determination to live.

The Pallbearer

After the bank fiasco I channeled my efforts toward accumulating funds for a farm wagon that I had seen attractively pictured in the Sears Roebuck catalog at a price of $7.00. Its dimensions were about five feet long and thirty inches high.

Having no desire to trust commercial banks again, I heard

MY SAVINGS GOAL

A Full Bank

that the People's Savings Bank of Alpena was issuing small individual savings banks. I got one and found that not only could it be fed change, but that a round hole was provided to accomodate rolled-up currency. Thus I began the long climb back to financial solvency with myself in total control. I added selling the "Saturday Evening Post" and "Collier's" magazines to my thrift stamp route, and each Wednesday evening would report to my father my sales successes or failures for the day.

One evening my report was so poor that my father couldn't believe it. Later, during a prayer meeting attended by some twenty neighbors, he asked me again how many stamps I had sold. When my reply was "None," the next question was, "Didn't Stewart McNeil (always a faithful buyer) buy some?" I answered, "No." "What did he say?" asked my father. "He said that he was flatter than piss on a plate," I replied quite truthfully. That night after the prayer meeting we had another session.

Persistence paid off and finally I filled my savings bank and took it to the People's Savings Bank to be opened by one of the tellers who had the key. The expectation was that the money would then be deposited in the Bank. Little did the banker know that my plan was to take the money straight away and buy the farm wagon. I could hardly wait for my bank to be opened because I had rolled my first dollar bill up and carefully slid it into the opening provided. Each week I had shaken the bank hard to determine how much it was filling up.

The trip to Alpena to meet the banker and have the bank opened was a high point in my life. My father had advised me to deposit the money in the bank and shortly thereafter, like the next day, to check it out, for then I would have my own checkbook.

As it turned out, there were sufficient funds to buy the wagon, but my enthusiastic shaking of the bank had caused the coins to shred my precious dollar bill into small unsalvageable pieces so that I never did realize the thrill of spending my first dollar!

Saving for the wagon until I finally had enough to pay for it, and ordering it from the Sears Roebuck catalog was a most satifying experience for one who was definitely goal-oriented. The day my father and I picked up the wagon at the Lachine railroad station was another high point, as was assembling and admiring it when the job was completed. The red wooden wheels, single trees and tongue complemented the green wagon box.

The Farm Wagon

I quickly pulled my new wagon to the neighboring McArthur farm and showed it off to Charlotte and Lucille who were about the same age as my sister and me. A bright idea, that didn't appear to be that bright later, came to me as we returned to our place. I decided to harness two of our calves, which were old hands at being harnessed and ridden, and take the McArthur girls for a ride. Charlotte refused to get in so Lucille and I took off down the road. The calves started well but for some reason suddenly bolted and Lucille and I soon found ourselves being hurled through the air. She grabbed a nearby woven wire fence and I was thrown to the ground. Although I was not seriously injured, I could hear the calves bawling as they distributed pieces of my new farm wagon along a quarter-mile length of road. My pride was damaged, but not so much as the wagon.

That evening I had another meeting with my father who tried to explain to me that one had to use judgment when putting expensive equipment at risk. Although I questioned his judgment at times, I was learning that his kindness was accompanied by a keen understanding of the fact that children were not little adults, but needed counsel when critical situations arose.

The BB Gun

Just prior to this incident Father had succumbed to my request for an air rifle that shot BB's. No doubt the price was low, but to part with funds that were needed elsewhere was certainly a sacrifice for him. Anxious to use my new gun, I read that the air to force out the BB was compressed by holding the stock in one hand and the barrel in the other and then folding the rifle over the knee to cock it. In doing so, however, I caught my forefinger between the barrel and the stock and cut out a sizeable piece of flesh. Although this was difficult to do, I managed to accomplish it.

When my father noticed the blood flowing, he asked me how I had done it. He didn't buy my explanation that I had caught it on one of the steel straps that bound the wooden barrel we used to collect rainwater, so another meeting was held. I told him how it happened and he told me that it wasn't necessary to lie to him. Further, he said that the gun was mine to keep, and that my own carelessness was the problem. He explained that there would be many more times when I would be tempted to lie, but that it would always be easier to live with telling the truth.

The Mare and Colt

It was a few weeks later that one of our mares gave birth to a colt. At the supper table my father told me that mother horses are very protective of their young and that he didn't want me to go into the field where she had the colt under surveilance. This warning was a challenge to me and after supper I slipped away to visit the alleged protector and her foal. As I viewed the newborn, a vicious mother leaped over the bushes, sank her teeth into my skull and rudely shifted me away from her pride and joy. As I ran the quarter of a mile to the barn where my father was milking, I experienced difficulty slowing the flood of blood flowing from the newly created holes in my scalp.

As I remember, my father told me to shut up and to quit crying. He studied my wounds and called for my mother to help him. Another horse, without a colt to protect, was quickly hitched to the buggy and off we went to Dr. Purdy's office which was located a mile away in Long Rapids. It was a unique experience to have a blind doctor sew up my scalp as my folks used cotton swabs to absorb the blood.

Very little conversation took place on the way home, and my father postponed the meeting regarding the incident until the next day. The injury didn't seem to have had any permanent effect except for a very uneven skull, which I still notice when I comb my hair.

Our Family, the Roots of my Education

MY FATHER

My father, David McConnell, was born in Ripley, Ontario, Canada, October 16, 1883 and died March 10, 1943 in Long Rapids. His parents were John McConnell and Catherine McDonald. They immigrated to Alpena when my father was four years old and later moved to the Bear Creek area near Lachine, just up the road from Long Rapids, where they established the family farm and later built the house in which we lived before our own was built.

Father told about the early days when supplies had to come from Detroit to Alpena by boat and how one spring when ice delayed the boat's arrival, the family had to dig up its seed potatoes for food to eat.

His Influence

Father taught me that if one wanted a satisfactory life, it would take some education plus a lot of luck, and that it was easy to close the door on both. I knew when I was very young that Father realized it took more that his fifth-grade education and a small sub-marginal farm to provide the satisfactory self-image and family style he desired. Buying the farm and tying himself down with a family had pretty much ruled out the element of luck for Father. I remember him one winter taking a short course to improve his reading and mathematics skills at Ferris Institute, now a state college, in Big Rapids, Michigan. In spite of his limited formal schooling, he was a well-educated man. He also was skilled with sick and injured animals. Had he the necesary education he could have been a veterinarian.

My father was progressive and often not too practical. For example, he purchased one of the first mechanical potato planters, hay loaders, corn harvesters and manure spreaders in the area. The income from the farm didn't pay for this equipment. I soon began to realize that bankers were not making social calls when they came to see the used farm machinery and obtain my father's signature on a piece of paper they referred to as a personal note that had expired and needed his signature to renew for another ninety days.

On those occasions I was unhappy with the lot of my father, and impressed by the clothes worn by the bankers as well as the wealth they exhibited by owning, or at least driving, an automobile.

Father and Mother, circa 1906

Posen Fire

My sister, Isabelle, tells that once our father collected a group of men to help fight the fire which was spreading rapidly in the timber near the small town of Posen which was about ten miles away. Before leaving he instructed Mother that if the smoke got so thick she couldn't see the neighboring houses, she should take a wash boiler full of family pictures, "little Jimmy" and Isabelle across the road to the center of a five-acre plowed field. Isabelle recalls climbing the stairs with Mother to the second story of our house to peer out the window at the approaching fire. Although several lives were lost, the fire did not reach our house.

Father was always able to respond to my questions. One day I noticed that most of our cows were standing up in the barnyard and I asked him why. He said that the cows knew it was going to rain. A few days later I pointed out to him that half of the cows were lying down while the others were standing. He answered that half of the cows were wrong. Years later in an arid part of California where it never rains in the summer I saw all of the cows in a barnyard standing and finally realized that my father had been pulling my leg.

MY MOTHER

Mother, Fannie Berthia McNeil, was born November 18, 1879 in a log cabin in Long Rapids, Michigan Township and died in Long Rapids July 7, 1958. Her father, David McNeil, of Scottish descent, was born in Antrim County, Ireland and migrated to Canada with his father and stepmother. He married Mother's mother (Isabell Ross) in Canada and then moved to Alpena and took out a homestead in Long Rapids. While the family stayed in Alpena, Grandfather walked the 18 miles to the homestead each week and built the cabin in which Mother was born and lived for 20 years.

Mother and Father were married May 23, 1906. She weighed only 90 pounds at the time. In Mother's memoirs, where she extolled the virtues of each of her children, is a cryptic sentence about me. "The next year Jimmy was born—May 26, 1908. He was a nice fat baby and David was so proud of him."

A Practical Person

My mother was a practical person. She full-well realized, as shiny new farm equipment was purchased, that the day of settlement would come too soon, and without the help of a miracle, even partial payments would be difficult to make.

Today we would refer to this predicament as the result of a negative cash flow. To me then it seemed to be a situation that bordered on poverty. In fact, our family was in an inservice training program for the great depression. When it came the pain of that experience was hardly noticed.

Although Mother was not overly religious, she was a faithful church goer and always carried more than her share of church responsibilities. She furnished items for church sales and socialized at the quilting parties that took place at the homes of members of the church and Sunday school support groups.

MY SIBLINGS

My sister and brothers contributed much to my personal development. Together with my parents they provided a warm, supportive family that overlooked my many shortcomings and applauded my successes.

Although I was the oldest boy in the family, sister Isabelle was the oldest child, having been born on February 26, 1907. A brother who only lived ten days was born June 23, 1913. Brother John was born January 3, 1915 in Alpena and Lloyd on March 3, 1919.

Isabelle is much like my mother—thoughtful and conscientious. I don't remember her as a child for she always seemed to me to be a young lady. She followed the teaching profession and helped the family financially during the dark days of the depression.

John, Jim, Lloyd and Isabelle, 1914

Sister Isabelle

Isabelle attended Alpena County Normal, taught at the Koline one-room school in Wellington Township and graduated from Central Michigan Teachers College with her Life Certificate.

She always was ready to do more than her share at community social gatherings. Because of her high school and college experiences her presence was a plus for the community.

Isabelle once worked at a summer resort. When the employer moved to Florida, she worked for his family there and became the first member of our family to have experiences in another state. That interested me especially when she said, "Many of the residents of Florida never have experienced snow."

Isabel Walcutt honored by Farm Bureau

By BETTY WERY
Herald-Leader Correspondent

Few people have contributed so extensively or achieved a more noteworthy volunteer record for the Menominee County Farm Bureau than has Isabel Walcutt of Daggett.

She may be a bit shy of publicity and the limelight, but she is not fearful about going all out for community involvement; and has given this top priority in her life.

Caring is not work to Isabel, it is charter members. The "Cloverleaf Group," to which they belonged was composed of several bachelors and others with small homes, "so we have many opportunities to host our local group," she said. This continued for a few years until the group disbanded. They later joined the Longrie Group, west of Stephenson, and she continued to be a member after Lester's death in 1973.

Soon other extracurricular activities were added, such as being secretary of the group; and be interested in."

Isabel's sense of humor and deep spirituality combine to make her inspiring as well as interesting. She maintains a fine balance between stern firmness and loving concern, so essential for good leadership. She is a member of the Daggett Moravian Church and Women's Fellowship.

Another club of which she is a member is called CCC or Community Charity Circle. This group of local women, and others interested, more than the girls did. I have always found working with young people enjoyable."

Isabel has five grown children. Jim and Shannon have lived in Alaska for several years. Jim works with F.A.A. and Shannon is retired from the Air Force. Another son, Bob, is a captain in the Air Force, stationed in England. Daughter Suzanne is a home economics teacher in the Dowagiac School System. Another daughter, Sally,

Brother John has a superb disposition. As a child he enjoyed every day, but was not enthusiastic about farming. I remember father assigning him the task of harvesting a crop of rutabagas. John decided after pulling a few of them that it would require less bending over if he drove a nail through a three-foot long pole to make a pry bar. He would push the nail into a rutabaga and force it from the ground with much less effort on his part.

Brother John

That evening my father met with John for a long session on the damage his creativity had done to the unsaleable wagon load of rutabagas. I was somewhat pleased, because for the first time the blame for wrongdoings was on someone besides me.

John had musical talent. He could play practically any musical instrument, while I could not play any—not even a mouth organ. He also excelled in dancing and acting which resulted in his taking leading roles in dramatic productions in high school and college.

His Talent

When John graduated from Central Michigan I was slightly irritated for as I perceived it, he was not educated to do anything. He had not pursued courses that qualified him to teach school. This was a false evaluation on my part for with John's personality, talents and ability he has been able to do much better than he probably would have done, had he chosen the field of education.

John was a born salesman but he made few promises to his prospective clients. He said that he always remembered the vacuum cleaner salesman who called on one of the farm women to sell a vacuum cleaner. As she opened the door, he pushed her aside, placed the vacuum cleaner in the middle of the room and took a couple of handfuls of dry horse manure from a sack and immediately started throwing it on the carpet. As she looked on with astonishment and horror, he said, "Relax, lady, this vacuum cleaner will clean this rug much cleaner than it was before, and if it doesn't, I promise to get down on my hands and knees and eat everything I'm putting on this beautiful carpet of yours." As she rushed to the kitchen he asked why she was leaving and not observing how the sweeper worked. She answered that she was going after the salt shaker, because the house was not wired for electricity.

Brother Lloyd

My father usually referred to Lloyd as the one who knew what to do. He completed high school with good grades and with more of a bent toward farming than either John or I. He could study a problem of practically any magnitude in a mechanical or general farm area and arrive at a workable solution.

Lloyd had many of the characteristics of my father. He was the first one out with his tractor and snow plough to clear the driveways for the elderly people in Long Rapids who had to have access to the community to pursue their daily activities.

Although I was eleven years older I always felt that many years younger than Lloyd when we approached various mechanical tasks on the farm. Lloyd's success gave me a better appreciation of a statement my father made one day as we were repairing a piece of farm equipment. "Jim, you had better go to college for you will never make it working with your hands."

Although Lloyd could do anything on the farm he recognized the financial limitations that faced all of us. He was the first one in line when he heard about the need for census takers for the 1940 U.S. Census. He and John also took advantage of the rural electrification projects when they were introduced to Northern Michigan. John would price and sell the jobs of wiring the houses and barns for electricity and Lloyd would do the installation.

Potato Bugs

It was early in his life that I detected that Lloyd was a good listener and would act immediately on what he felt was a proper response to a problem. In the potato country in which we lived one of the enemies of a successful crop was the potato bug. It seemed to me that from some well-located vantage point the bugs would observe us planting potatoes and soon after the plants started to grow they would descend en masse and devour the leaves within hours. Arsenic of lead was the only deterrent available at that time, but a sudden rain after spraying would wash off the poison with the result that the bugs were not killed.

Lloyd to the Rescue

Lloyd had listened to the various family conversations regarding the potato bug problem and decided at the early age of four to carry out his own solution. With a quart fruit jar in hand he systematically, row by row, picked the potato bugs from the leaves and put them in the jar. He had successfully filled one jar and was heading for the house to get another empty one when I encountered him and asked what he was doing. He explained his plan and informed me that he was saving money for our father who would pay him one cent for every bug. From my 15-year old vantage point I laughingly told him that Father would not pay him for the bugs and went on to my own work. Soon Lloyd came up to me with the empty jar. When I questioned him about what happened to the contents he informed me that he had released them!

This experience brought home to me that young as Lloyd was he partially understood the concept of payment for services rendered. I also learned that one should weigh carefully statements made when convers-

ing with children. Adults can usually detect when one is speaking in jest, but children react seriously.

Fantasy World

Everyone's mind works differently. I never was much of a person to indulge in fantasy, but Lloyd was. I would often find him a mile or more from home walking along a side road or a creek. As we would return home he would reveal to me outlandish stories about a make-believe family. Hissing was the family name and he always referred to their home as Hissin's house. He was a little mixed up about how this family fit into his life, but he never had any doubt of its existence.

Lloyd suffered from heart and circulatory problems that contributed to his early death, April 7, 1970.

PARENTAL SUPPORT

The importance of education was recognized and emphasized by both parents whenever a situation presented itself that would serve as an example. For inspiration they stressed the fate that had befallen local people of practically every age group whose lack of education contributed to their problems.

My mother never forgot to mention the monetary advantages of having an education. She realized that with only an eighth grade education most doors to opportunity were closed, so high school attendance for all four children in the family was a foregone conclusion.

I don't think that education beyond the eighth grade originally appealed to me because of my desire to seek more knowledge. It was the potential monetary advantages that attracted my attention. I daily saw examples of the high correlation between continual poverty and little education. Men who visited our home wearing matching coats and pants had gone to high school and beyond.

I came home from school one day and saw a shiny black automobile in the front yard and a man standing in the middle of a ten-acre field of peas. I hurried out to learn that the visitor was our first county agriculture agent, Harold Sheets, who had come to discuss the plight of the pea crop with my father. The aphids were in the process of devouring our most cherished cash crop for that year. I was saddened by the news of the aphids but impressed by the visitor's well-tailored three-piece herringbone suit.

The County Agent

Although I was only twelve or so, I quickly found out that his next stop was the Behling farm a mile away. He agreed to take me with him, providing a walk home would not be objectionable. While riding in his Monroe automobile over the dirt road, I gleaned the fact that he had gone to college and had just returned from Russia where he had been helping the Russians start a five-year agricultural improvement program. I made great time returning on foot from the Behlings, convinced more than ever that a high school education would not be sufficient and that college was a must for me.

As soon as I returned home, I located Russia in my sixth grade geography book. This was almost as thrilling an experience as having the opportunity to ride in an automobile and to meet a man who had gone to college and was making a living in agriculture, and wore a three-piece suit.

Is High School Possible?

Although my parents were impressed with my new enthusiasm about continuing education beyond the eighth grade, they reminded me that the distance between our home and Alpena where a four-year high school was located, was a substantial barrier. Not having an automobile, or much prospect of ever having one, was going to present some problems. Money appeared to be one of the key ingredients that would be required to help fulfill my newly acquired desire. My grades were only fair, but I felt that I could pass the county eighth grade examination when the time came.

As I worked my way up the lockstep ladder toward the eighth grade, I never forgot that money was crucial to my goals. Unfortunately, I seemed sometimes to have more trouble hanging on to money than I did in getting it in the first place. My sister and I had sold two bushels of crab apples to Mr. Sloan, the village blacksmith, and each of us received ten cents. I lost my ten cents on the way home and whenever I drive that mile today I wonder how I could have been so careless.

THE NEW SCHOOL

A new four-room school was built a half mile closer to Long Rapids just as I was about to enter the eighth grade. This school was a first for Long Rapids township for it provided opportunities for children in the community to complete two years of high school. It was the first school to offer more than eight years of schooling in the county, other than the high school in Alpena.

Beginning the eighth grade in a new school was indeed a thrill. Although the seats were screwed to the floor and had been used by some city children prior to being moved to our new school, they were single seats. This was my first experience of being assigned a piece of my own real estate for the next nine months.

I appreciated the facts that the new building site was closer to home and that I was separated from the little children as the first four grades were in a separate room.

In general, things seemed to be falling in place, although my thrift stamp government representative position had come to an abrupt stop when World War I ended. My ego was inflated when I learned that I had sold the most stamps and was awarded a gold and silver drinking cup. It had hinged handles that clamped around the cup and an all-leather case. I kept it at school where I could take it out of my desk and admire it. Later, when the new school burned to the ground in a somewhat mysterious fire, my silver and gold drinking cup burned with it.

Shinny Star

The new school had a site that permitted us to play my favorite game, Shinny. It was played with a very crude hockey stick, having a small piece of tree root as the head, and a

38

four-foot length of trunk as the shaft. The puck varied from a tin can to a piece of hardwood tree root cut into a 3" x 3" cube that could withstand a severe blow from the shinny stick and still maintain its original shape. To play shinny, you first drew a line across the middle of a field and then one player would hit the puck across and try to prevent his opponent from returning it across the line.

After a few weeks I was becoming recognized as a worthy opponent and was challenged to a game by Nelson Thomson. My first drive was a super one, but ended in tragedy. The puck hit Nelson squarely in the mouth and broke off one of his front teeth. A meeting was called with Nelson, my dad and Mr. Thomson. It was decided that shinny would be banned and that we would confine our play activities to tag, hide and seek, and other such unadventurous games.

Agnes Portwine was one of my better teachers. I remember little about the academic things she taught, but she furnished something special that we all needed at the time. She was kind, informative and always had a smile on her face. I have always been thankful that she was our teacher that year. **Miss Portwine**

Another memorable figure of that period was our new County Superintendent of Schools, Earl Gates. He did more than drop by and see the teacher. Mr. Gates took time to talk to the students as a group, and he also talked with us individually. He learned of our personal interests and commended those who would attend high school.

Mr. Gates elevated the education profession in my mind by replacing the horse and buggy with a Model-T Ford that sported a box on the back for transporting books and supplies. The other thing I remember about him is that his wife was blind. Even as a boy, I always thought that he had problems that were most trying and I felt very sad for him. **Mr. Gates**

1922—A MEMORABLE YEAR

The year, 1922, was memorable as it was then that we were able to buy our first automobile—a Model-T Ford turtleback that could be equipped as a small pickup truck. Scraping the $400 together was a cooperative family project, as was convincing Father to buy it. He had been critical of Willie Hall who had purchased a Model-T Ford sedan the year before and referred to it as Willie's lap dog kennel.

By this time I fancied myself as knowledgeable about Model-T's for I had assisted the Jim Thomson family with jacking up their Model-T sedan after each venture on the road. This exercise resulted in keeping the weight off the tires and supposedly lengthened their life.

Father, Mother and Lloyd, 1923

The County Exam

1922 was also the year I finished the eighth grade and drove the car to Alpena to write the county examination which permitted me to gain entrance to high school. Things were looking up, for two years of high school could be acquired in the new school in Long Rapids. I passed the examination, but not with flying colors. My average of 78% was acceptable but the 61% in reading and 60% in history were on the borderline since a minimum of 60% in each subject was required. I have often wondered what my life would have been like if I had received 59% in history.

Years later, when county examinations for rural students were eliminated, a major discrimination against rural youth was removed. Evidence was growing that rural children lacked opportunities equal to those of city children. Most of the rural teachers, for example, could not qualify to teach in city schools. It was necessary for country children to furnish their own transportation, which prevented most of them from attending high school.

Most of us are capable of learning more, thinking more, and doing more than we do. Often times or we come up with excuses in an attempt to shift the blame for our modest accomplishments. Like the two crows who were sitting on a fence watching a jet plane take off. One said to the other, "Boy, I wish I could fly that fast." The second replied, "I know I could do that if I had four rear ends and they were all on fire!"

It often pays to be flexible, even if you are quite certain that you are right. My father used to repeat this little poem, found on a tombstone:

Here lies the Body of Solomon Day,
Who died maintaining the right of way.
He was right, dead right, as he drove along;
But he is just as dead as if he had been wrong.

I never tell people about my troubles. Over the years I have learned that half of them don't give a damn, and the other half are pleased as punch.

PERCENTAGE ATTAINED AT EXAMINATION ALPENA COUNTY MICH.

Name: *James McConnell*
Date: 5-20-22

Arithmetic	84
Civil Government	89
Geography	80
Grammar	81
Orthography and Spelling	84
Course of Study	
Penmanship	86
Physiology	73
Reading	61
School Law	
Theory and Art	
U. S. History	60
Agriculture	90
Algebra	
Botany	
General History	
Physics	
Geometry	
Institute	
Average Standing	78

Diploma Later

STANDING ADOPTED BY THE BOARD
EIGHTH GRADE--Minimum required 60 per cent.
General average not less than 75 per cent.
THIRD GRADE--Minimum required 60 per cent.
General average not less than 80 per cent.
SECOND GRADE--Minimum required 70 per cent.
General average not less than 85 per cent.
INSTITUTE CREDITS--For full attendance during the entire continuance of the Institute per cent.

The High School Years

My eighth grade had been spent in the new four-room school in Long Rapids. Although most pupils wish to move on to another building when they enter high school, I was satisfied to go upstairs where all subjects were taught to ninth and tenth graders.

Only about twenty students made up the entire population of our high school and the curriculum was exclusively limited to academic studies. There were no athletic programs, clubs nor activities of any kind.

All students left for home at four o' clock to help with the routine chores in the houses or on the farms.

George King Our teacher was George King. I never knew what credentials he had but I did know that he must have been a genius to have taught such a wide range of subjects. In the ninth grade the curriculum included English, History, Physiology, Algebra and Botany. No doubt he taught most of those, plus others, to the tenth grade as well.

Mr. King was a young man. He roomed and boarded at the Boorst residence in Long Rapids—a long, green, one-story building that housed the local pool hall as well as the Boorsts. I have often thought about the long, lonely evenings that he must have spent that year. We had him to our home a few times, as did some other families, but there just couldn't have been much opportunity for him to do anything but remain in his room at the Boorsts.

The Fire My high school education in Long Rapids was cut short a few months after beginning. A fire burned our new school to the ground in January, 1923, and for the remainder of the year classes were held in makeshift rooms around town.

In later years I realized that it was pure luck that the fire took place when the ground was frozen—for this assured that the school site was saved. What brought this to mind was a night I spent in a hotel in Sault St. Marie, Michigan, where the local newspaper was harrassing the fire department about a downtown fire the night before. The headline read: "Another Fire Destroys Major Downtown Building; Lot Saved."

The fire was a blow to my family as well as to the other families that had students attending the school. It could have been a blessing in disguise, however. When I later entered high school in Alpena, I discovered that our teacher in Long Rapid was not as well prepared in certain subjects, such as algebra, as were the teachers in the six-hundred pupil high school in Alpena. Although my early mathematics deficiencies carried through my life, I have always been grateful to George King for the windows he opened to me in other areas.

Although Mr. King was responsible for teaching subjects that he had not majored in, there were few ill effects on me. Later in my teaching career I found myself in the same situation. Most of us are ignorant in many areas, even though we show no inhibitions in discussing subjects and events widely. If books, pictures and other media are available in a school the non-knowledgeable teacher can become a resource person and introduce students to the avenues through which they can study independently.

We had few books available in our school, but I did read about Abraham Lincoln's desire to learn and the failures experienced by Thomas Edison. To this day I feel that the inspiration generated by the teacher is as important as the knowledge he or she has of the subject matter. Many brass rings pass by, and the ability of a teacher to stimulate a student to grab a few makes the difference.

SIMPLE PLEASURES

Beyond school and chores, our lives had only a few, simple diversions. Radios may have been common elsewhere, but like electricity, they did not become available in our family until I was well into my teen years. Radio did provide an incentive to complete the chores early, which could push supper ahead an hour or so and free the family to listen to favorite programs.

There were no playing cards in our home, since they were seen to be closely associated with gambling and drinking, but one Christmas our cousins brought us a game called "A.D.T. Messenger Boy." The game was played by moving figures around a square surface and the winner was determined by the number of points collected by the messenger. Although it didn't require much thought and skill, it was important to me because it provided an incentive to get out of the barn and into the house to participate in something that was not a bit like work.

Limited transportation handicapped dating but I did manage to get around to some of the community social activities. The Saturday night square dances at Lachine were especially interesting. There were quantities of liquor consumed by some on those occasions, and now and then a brawl would attract a considerable number away from the dance floor as the evening went on.

Dancing Shoes

House parties were more to my liking and I found myself learning square dance calls and enjoying the dances a lot. Since farm shoes were not conducive to fancy stepping, I went to Reeder's Shoe Store in Alpena and purchased my first pair of oxfords. They were crepe soled, and so weren't really dancing shoes. They cost $3.50 and I wore them for the first time at a party at the Larmer farm house just north of Long Rapids. I took Kathleen Niergarth and we danced to a tune that was new to me: "It's Three O' Clock in the Morning."

For some reason, those house parties held a higher priority for me than the spin the bottle parties sponsored by the Sunday School.

ALPENA HIGH SCHOOL

The fire that burned down our local school could have ended my high school education and started my farming career but for my parents' strong feeling on the importance of education. It was decided that my sister Isabelle and I would transfer to Alpena High School, some eighteen miles away. Transportation would be by our family Model-T Ford—at least until the snows came—with the understanding that I got home in time to do my share of the farm chores.

Enrolling in the Alpena High School was an awesome experience. There were more students and teachers than I had ever seen before. Although there were few curriculum decisions to be made, Latin definitely appeared to be one of the offerings to be declined. Agriculture was chosen as a winner. Although I definitely did not want to be a farmer, the memory of the county agent with his pressed suit and shiny automobile influenced me to take that course. Typing, English and French were also among the subjects I chose. French didn't prove to be one of my better decisions, since many deficiencies in spoken and written English needed my attention.

Alpena High School

I suspect that the French teacher had not achieved total proficiency in the language herself, and I never did acquire a keen interest in it. I do recall that the title of the textbook was "La Tosh du Petit Pierre," or "The Task of Little Peter," At the end of the year I could pronounce the name of the book with some degree of accuracy but beyond that my comprehension of the language was unimpressive.

I soon began to realize that it would be necessary for me either to start from scratch with mathematics or to deal with it, catch as catch can, as the need arose. Having no desire to start all over again, I chose the latter and ever since those high school days, have struggled with any complicated aspects of mathematics.

Mathematics

My background in algebra was limited to the knowledge I had acquired from Mr. King, who had had his own problems with Algebra I at Long Rapids. Consequently, Algebra II put me in the same position as our neighbor's dog, Chaucer, when he pursued a porcupine. Chaucer knew that he could kill it if he only could figure out a way to get hold of it.

And Other Subjects

Mr. Reed, the physics teacher, opened some new doors for me when he demonstrated that heat loss could actually be measured. He also made me realize the necessity of precision in all forms of measurement. This gave me an insight into why some of the farm buildings I had helped construct had not come out square when I had set forms for the foundation merely by pacing the distance a couple of times.

Typing was a course that did as much for me as any subject I ever took in that it made it possible to speed up the process of putting my thoughts on paper. No matter how I tried, my handwriting always slowed me down so that I often lost a thought between the time an idea entered my head and the time I could write it down.

In agriculture class, the stress on soil testing, rotating crops, planting proper seed and selecting registered livestock for breeding purposes gave me insights as to why some farmers were successful and others were not. Up until that time, I believed the story about the farmer who asked his neighbor how he should spend the $10,000 he had inherited, and was told that he should just keep on farming until it was all gone.

Adjustment

In spite of entering Alpena High School as a sophomore, I soon worked into the routine. There were a number of rural students from other townships in the county, and the city students were helpful to us.

Farm boys were thought to be more responsible than those from the city, many of whom had few if any chores at home. This probably was the reason that the Superintendent of Schools, Mr. Curtis, once met me coming down the stairs of the school, and told me that there was a fire in the school tower. He asked me to get his car out of the basement. Having had no experience with a gear shift car, I quickly drove it into a concrete wall, thereby winning the distinction of being responsible for the major casualty of the fire in the tower.

As winter of 1923-24 approached, driving or carpooling with other students from Long Rapids terminated as snow made driving an impossibility. So, at the age of fifteen, I had to find board and room in Alpena.

Alpena was controlled in those days by a few people, among whom were members of the Richardson, Fletcher, Holmes, Harris and Gilchrist families. My sister, Isabelle, was successful in securing a part-time, live-in job babysitting and doing housekeeping for the Gilchrists. I was fortunate in getting work before and after school with the Phillip Fletcher and Clinton Harris families. Both residences were on State Street, only four blocks apart. All homes located on the east side of State Street backed up to Lake Huron where ample beach front provided space for owners to exercise their highly bred German Shepherd dogs. I soon learned that a State Street address was a symbol of living in the high rent district of Alpena.

Mrs. Jake Gray agreed to provide a room and an occasional meal for $5.00 per week. Furnace stoking, lawn work, dog washing and occasional chauffeuring occupied would-be leisure time. I attended a few basketball games, but the first football game I saw was during my second year in college.

Living at the Gray residence ended after my sophomore year and I obtained space at the Gammage residence and did some chauffeuring for a Mrs. Gordon, who prepared breakfasts for professional people who worked in the area. It was my first experience at seeing a long table of grapefruit halves set out in the winter months when no one was ill!

My sophistication in driving automobiles also broadened. I soon was driving a Dodge Brothers as well as an air-cooled Franklin, a Cadillac and a Packard. All four cars had different gear shift systems. At that time I probably could have driven Superintendent Curtis's Oldsmobile out of the basement without wrecking it.

The various jobs in Alpena kept me from visiting my parents very often. When I did so on an occasional weekend,

Work-Study Plan

JDM, circa 1923

Chauffeuring

it was difficult for me when it was time to return to Alpena on Sunday afternoon. I knew that Mother and Father were sacrificing by doing the farm work that I would have done if I were at home. At times, I suggested that I not go back to school, but neither of them would hear of it.

EXTRA-CURRICULAR ACTIVITIES

High school is supposed to be the time for getting acquainted with girls, widening spheres of acquaintances, and more or less launching into adulthood. This was not the case for me as my schedule was almost all study and work. A couple of broadening experiences, did occur, however.

Chauffeuring my employers and their families to the train station or helping them prepare for a trip to warmer climates were vicarious experiences. But the occasions I cherished most were when opportunities allowed me to leave the area. A trip with the Glee Club to Mt. Pleasant, Michigan, the home of Central State Teachers College was one of those celebrated occasions. That I was a member of the Glee Club is evidence that there wasn't much competition to join. My father stopped at one of my job sites the night before I was to leave and gave me all of the money he had, about two dollars.

The Hummer

The hundred and fifty mile bus trip was a new experience. As we traveled along the highway in our singing caravan, I realized that most of those aboard had much more musical talent than I. I wisely decided to hum along and not be responsible for leading my colleagues off key when the contests took place during the next two days.

Our group didn't win any of the competitions but I had an opportunity to observe campus achievers wearing white sweaters with big felt "C's" sewn on them. I soon became dedicated to the cause of being an achiever in something and being recognized as such by others. Underneath, I wanted to accomplish something of which I could be proud and which would partially compensate my parents who were sacrificing in order that I could have opportunities to succeed.

Attending college seemed even more of a necessity than it had prior to the trip with the Glee Club.

The Church Rally

One other trip added to my desire to become an ex-resident of Alpena County. I was a representative of a Congregational Church youth group and attended a regional rally at the state capital in Lansing. We met in a huge auditorium and had our picture taken on the lawn of the capitol building. I had learned that by standing at one end of the group when the picture was being taken and running fast enough to the other end of the group so as to exceed the speed of the camera sweep I could appear at both ends of the picture. I won a questionable notoriety by accomplishing that feat.

There was much singing and praying throughout the sessions. I accepted the Lord and denounced the devil in unison with hundreds of other youth, anticipating that by making a favorable report back home I would be selected as a representative for the next conference.

The Finger Bowl

We were farmed out to different homes for meals and lodging. I drew a childless family that was not only religious, but rich, and accustomed to the finer ways of living. I was introduced not only to embroidered placemats, but to finger bowls. The water with lemon sections added a flavor to the water that I had not experienced up to that time. My drinking the contents probably would have gone by without incident but when I asked for a refill, the hostess alerted me to the intended purpose of the finger bowl. Although I was treated with kindness and an air of sympathy, the evidence of my social upbringing slightly tainted my welcome.

At times I may have questioned the value of the high school as part of the total educational process, but at present I favor our current organization plan for educating youth. I would stress, however, the point that high school should present opportunities for youth to have new experiences outside the classroom. I shudder when I hear about parents hurrying their children through worthwhile new experiences in order to get them back to school on time. A couple of days at EPCOT, or Disney

World or a first class museum would set a learning level for children and adults that most schools would find difficult to meet.

All Work...   Except for these interludes my time was spent studying, attending classes and working to remain in high school. At that stage in my life I should have been learning to have some fun, enjoy friends, participate in sports and select some life-long leisure activities. I regret that this did not happen. I never was athletic but have always felt that I would have enjoyed the various athletic activities had I had an opportunity to participate in some of them. At least I could have established some preferences and no doubt would have had more sympathy for the participants when, with their apparent easy efforts, they fail to achieve their desired goals.

No doubt this situation contributed to my never having had a date while in Alpena High School and the fact that I skipped all of my class reunions until the 50th arrived. I guess it took me that long to prove to myself that although I was a country boy I eventually was able to become comfortable in social gatherings of my peers.

Although my work-study program was not ideal, it did give me an opportunity to observe men who were successful in life, or who were fortunate enough to have been born into families whose forebears were successful. Most of the wealth in Alpena was in the hands of not more than a dozen families, and I occupied a grandstand seat observing the great gap that existed between the haves and have-nots.

I felt that it was too bad that rich people died since they had so many more opportunities to enjoy themselves than poor folks. There was not sufficient evidence that when they died life after death would equal the present style of living to which they had become accustomed.

MY SENIOR YEAR   During my senior year my financial situation improved because of a new job washing and driving the Roy Richardson family Packards. It made it possible for me to purchase a portable Remington typewriter on the installment plan.

The highlight of my senior year began on Thanksgiving morning, 1925. I had just finished washing the third Packard when Roy Richardson, son of one of the early lumber kings in northern Michigan, came out of the house and inquired as to how I was going to spend Thanksgiving Day. When I told him that I would be staying around, he said, "Take the car and go home for Thanksgiving dinner." I did so and on arriving home created a dozen reasons to drive around Long Rapids to expose my newly acquired status symbol. That was one day when I experienced a mixture of admiration, respect, envy and pride—not only from my family—but from the entire community.

The Suits

Phillip Fletcher, who was part owner of the Alpena Power Company, proved to be one who was not only a good employer of high school students, but also a kind man and a keen observer. After watching me work his hunting dogs one day, he invited me to go up to his bedroom and try on some suits that were spread out on the bed. I, of course, pretended that even those that didn't fit suited me perfectly, and hurried home with a silk suit, a Harris tweed and two others that looked expensive. Eventually, I sold one that didn't fit too well to our part-time hired man and used the money to double up on my typewriter payments.

At last I was the proud owner of a three-piece suit—and everything matched. Today, if a man's coat and pants don't match, the wearer may still be rich. In those days, there was no such thing as coordinated fabrics, and the wearer of unmatched clothes was definitely poor.

One hears about the good old days, but as I compare my present wardrobe with the one I owned in 1925-26, these are the good days. I do feel, however, that my early experiences made me conscious of the importance of color and coordination, and the pleasure that can be derived from purchasing appropriate clothing for a variety of situations.

Phil Fletcher and his wife Katy will always retain a warm spot in my heart. Their desire to help the less fortunate gave me a new outlook on life. Up until that time I only saw wealthy people driving by in their

Cadillacs and Packards. I had heard that the Fletchers' wealth had not been earned, but inherited. Working for them I soon learned that having wealth didn't mean that they carried it with them; and that the wealthy have other problems. It became evident to me that problems are problems and learning that I was not the only one who had them gave me some consolation.

It also became evident that Katy did not have a great understanding of the time that it took to complete routine tasks that she assigned to me. She would be disappointed when I fell far short of removing a quarter of an acre of dandelions from her yard in a day's time. Yet she was astonished at my ability to treat her garden tools with rust preventative in the matter of minutes. Those experiences helped me later to understand and evaluate work loads that were assigned to me or that I assigned to others.

The Cement Works

Clinton Harris was one of the top executives of the Huron Portland Cement Company, and through his influence I secured employment at the plant during the summers of my last two years of high school.

Working at the plant, where hundreds of men were permanent employees, was another experience that made it easier for my parents and fellow workers to convince me that education and special training were essential to a young man with ambition to succeed. (I do mean "permanent" employees, because the cement dust on a sweaty man leaves a permanent impression.)

I was first assigned to the bag cleaning department. Before the advent of paper bags, cement was sold in cloth bags which were tied with a mechanical screwdriver-type device and filled through a slit in the bottom. After being emptied on the job, the sacks were returned to be retied and refilled. Our team received the bags as they left the cleaner. The rumor was that enough cement dust was reclaimed to pay the wages of all the workers in our department. I remember feeling that I personally stood in the way of that goal since I was breathing so much of the ill-gained profit. Washing windows at the cement plant was an unheard of activity. When the cement dust accumulated to the point that it reached a quarter of an inch, the windows were broken out and new glass installed.

Although my hair was brown at the time, it soon turned the color of cement. After trying to scrub the dust out a couple of times, I deleted that activity from my daily routine when I heard that my hair might set. The same thing happened when I tried to wash my clothes. My last message to my boss, Mr. Law, was written in cement dust on a cement table. It read, "I am grateful for your guidance and encouragement the past two summers. You have stimulated me to enroll in college this fall."

The money earned during those two summers at the cement plant helped replenish my wardrobe, finish paying for my typewriter and buy my parents a few things they needed. On June 20, 1926, I graduated from high school. My parents attended the graduation and were as proud as punch. I was not the valedictorian of the class, but neither was I the anchor man. Moreover, it was becoming clear to me that I was fast approaching the time in my life when some key decisions would have to be made.

AFTER HIGH SCHOOL

I had read several college catalogs and most of the course descriptions made college sound fairly unattractive. That of the School of Geology at the University of Michigan sounded interesting, however, so I wrote for information and subsequently enrolled in a short summer geology field trip by boat around the upper peninsula of Michigan. My father drove me to Mackinaw to meet the geology group, but we were a few minutes late arriving and I sadly watched the boat leaving the dock. The fact that I'm not a geologist today may well be attributed to my having missed the boat.

Wanderlust

At that time, of course, I had done very little traveling, but I still retained memories of automobiles going by our farm home, and I knew that there must be places that offered more experiences for me than Alpena had provided.

Although I was too busy to make many friends in high school, I did become acquainted with David Markham who was two or three years my senior. He worked as a teller in a downtown bank and was the proud owner of a new four-cylinder Henderson motorcycle with a sidecar.

The Trip West

My first chance for adventure came when Dave asked me to accompany him on a trip to the West Coast. He offered to furnish the transporation if I could help with the expenses. Since the vehicle consumed little fuel and we were camping out, it appeared to be a golden opportunity for me to get a look at the rest of the world.

Dave was the driver for the majority of the trip. From my vantage point in the sidecar, it appeared that all the major highways were in the process of either being built or repaired, and the surfacing being used was tar. Although I wore goggles, there was still sufficient face exposure to attract the bits of tar that were thrown from the front wheel. With the aid of the sun, those facial tar pits resulted in sores that lasted well into the next year.

Although the trip probably would have been more pain than pleasure for some, it was an event of a lifetime for me. Observing prairie dogs playing "chicken" as they waited until the last second before pulling their heads into their holes proved to be a time consuming pastime. Losing meals to the black bears in Yellowstone National Park could have been frightening had we realized the potential danger that existed.

Mechanical problems and dwindling funds took us no further west than Yellowstone Park. We decided to return via a southern route which led us through Pierre, South Dakota where an anxious automobile driver chose to pass us on a bridge and completely demolished the motorcycle. We sold the speedometer for $10.00 and hitchhiked into Chicago. A policeman on duty in the loop, after checking our credentials, bought our remaining source of protection from the wild animals and Indians of Wyoming and Montana, a 44-caliber revolver, and made it possible for us to eat as we hitchhiked to Alpena.

That trip convinced me that traveling could be fun but that experiences such as sleeping in a haystack in Minnesota and being awakened by a hissing sound that could have been a snake, lacked some of the comforts of home.

One hot day we stopped off along the road for a drink of water at a farm house and were told by a teenager that he was poor and asked us to give him some money. When I said, "Do you own this farm"? His answer was, "No, we're not that poor"!

Family Portrait, circa 1928. From left: John, James, Father, Mother, Lloyd and Isabelle

When travelling and dining out week after week I sometimes question the quality of the food and cleanliness in the kitchens. That's when I'm reminded of the four travelers who also had been experiencing some questionable food in their movements around the country. As the waiter approached their table they all expressed a desire for a glass of water and one of them who had become somewhat paranoid about cleanliness, said, "And I want my water in a clean glass." The waiter returned shortly with the four glasses balanced on a tray and said, "And which one of you wanted your water in a clean glass?"

55

Family gathering, 1940. Mother, Jim, Isabelle, John, Lloyd with nephew Jim Walcutt, and Father.

Alpena County Normal School, 1927 graduation class. MacConnell rear and center.

Learn, Earn, Learn, Improve

On graduating from high school I was attracted to a number of occupational fields, including geology, dentistry and medicine. I had a great deal of encouragement from my parents and some neighbors to aspire to higher education. It was great to hear adults express confidence in one, but it was frustrating to realize that though the possibilities were theoretically limitless, the probable realities were limited because of finances and ability. I fast faced reality and decided that my choice of a career would be limited to a profession that could be pursued in a piecemeal fashion such as teaching. Learn, earn, learn, improve, then earn more, was the course that was set for me.

THE COUNTY NORMAL SCHOOL

A county normal school had been established in Alpena on the second floor of the Bingham Grade School on Washington Avenue. I scheduled an interview with half of the faculty, Barbara Anthony, the principal, who was assisted by the other half, Alberta Dutton, the critic teacher. Although I let Mrs. Anthony know during the interview that I might not be going on to college, I realized full well that a year at the County Normal would give me a teaching certificate that would qualify me to teach school for three years without additional training. The going wage for such teachers was $100.00 per month for the nine-month school year. Earning a total of $2,700 over a three-year period seemed very attractive, especially since there were no other opportunities waiting in the wings. So I enrolled in September, 1926.

In later years I've often reflected that most of us make some good decisions during a lifetime. Deciding to attend Alpena County Normal School was probably the key decision that influenced my life and career. County Normal provided me some much needed windows at a time when blank walls were everywhere. Modest as it was, it was my springboard to opportunity.

The Faculty

Mrs. Barbara Anthony

Mrs. Anthony made it clear to me that English was a subject that would play a key role in my success not only as a teacher but as a person, and that others would be judging me by my ability to properly speak the English language. The ability to write and present subject matter clearly was also stressed. Probably the thing that impressed me most was that for the first time in my life, a bright, professional educator appeared to have confidence in me.

I found myself being intimidated by Mrs. Anthony, not because she was so bright but because I was dumb by comparison. I listened to her a lot. I learned that she had never gone to high school, and would not accept defeat in spite of adversities such as I would never have.

Barbara Anthony's scholastic achievements at Central Michigan State Teachers College at Mt. Pleasant intrigued me. I was further impressed when I learned of a repeated performance at the University of Chicago and at Columbia University where she excelled while earning her Master's Degree.

I had read about bright people, but meeting one who cared about people and stood ready to help was a real inspiration for me.

Miss Dutton, our critic teacher, conducted the practice teaching demonstrations, and also supervised the teacher training. In teaching a third grade class, I learned the advantage of work organization by preparing lesson plans and following them carefully.

A Quality Experience

The Normal class was small, and both Mrs. Anthony and Miss Dutton were good teachers. My practice teaching went well and my lesson plans seemed to be acceptable. Mrs. Anthony strengthened my English skills and made me aware of the advantages of having confidence in myself. I was selected for a role in the play, "Clarence," and was charged with the responsibility of organizing a number of off-campus educational and social activities.

The year went smoothly. My father had purchased a Model-T Ford sedan, with much encouragement from the family, which provided me occasional transportation. I was able to continue my part-time jobs around Alpena and the typewriter was paid off. I also became the proud owner of a tan three-piece suit.

I came to believe that the size of a college is secondary to the quality of the teaching, and the ability of the instructors to instill a sense of pride and self-confidence in the students. Both teachers at County Normal stressed the importance of presenting subject matter in a clear and meaningful way.

Colleagues

It would be difficult to measure the contribution my fellow students made to the various communities that employed them as they left school and became the educational leaders of rural schools. Most were responsible to a three-person district school board. The boards varied in quality as do boards of education today, but for the most part those board members were very limited in their formal education. Keeping school taxes as low as possible usually had high priority with them. Most of those schools now have been absorbed by community school districts that provide transportation as well as high school opportunities for all.

One of the board members of a country school expounded the virtues of a teacher who had, in his opinion, successfully completed her first year of teaching. His words of praise included the statement that she taught the whole nine months and used only one box of chalk! In those days, rural parents and children were engaged in a game of educational Russian roulette in reverse. The chances of having a good school year, during which learning and growth could take place, depended entirely upon whether or not there was a good teacher that year in the magazine of the educational pistol.

Lucky Lindy

Although graduation was the highlight of the year to us, some thought it was equalled by a radio broadcast on the evening of May 21, 1927, while we were having a graduation party at the Fox residence in Bolton. "Lindberg has successfully completed his solo flight from Roosevelt Field, New York, to Le Bourget, Paris, in 33 hours and 20 minutes," was the opening line of that news announcement.

Farewell, Normal

Although there were other normal schools in Northern Michigan, they were limited in number. For the most part they were the forerunners of Community Colleges. The latter, in my opinion, have been the unique contribution of the United States to higher education in the world. As they developed, the community colleges have been responsible for the continued education of thousands upon thousands of students. When Alpena County Normal was closed, the Alpena Community College was established and located on a sizeable site donated by Jesse Besser on Thunder Bay River.

To this day I never question that I chose the correct profession for me. It was while attending County Normal and during my first year of teaching that I became a realist and decided that excuses were not going to help me in pursuing a career. I realized that in order to be successful, one had to have an education, and be willing to produce work that was above average. I later recognized that one's success was often aided by people who have faith in you, along with the timing and luck to be in the right place at the right time.

MY FIRST PROFESSIONAL JOB

During my career I have interviewed for a position on only three occasions. My first interview was with the Long Rapids three-member school board. The interview was as short as the supply of qualified teachers. I was notified of my acceptance five minutes after the interview and, in the fall of 1927, began teaching in the school that replaced the structure that had burned when I was a student there.

As the head teacher of a two-room school, I was responsible for teaching all of the subjects in fifth, sixth, seventh and eighth grades. Mrs. Horton, the other teacher, had the first four grades. My parents' house was but a mile from the school so I lived at home. The playground consisted of a couple of acres of land. With my father's help we installed some swings for the students and a high school student from

Alpena painted the name of the school on a plank and mounted it over the front door. We tried to organize games such as baseball, and some others which were an improvement over the dangerous games I had played as a child at the Jones School.

Money for improvements of any kind was either scarce or non-existent. While teaching that first year, I discovered that our local institutions, including my school, were nearly as hard-pressed for money as I was personally. Yet, even at that, there was humor in the situation from time to time.

The Scottish descendants in the area were not noted for throwing money away. In fact they were known to carefully weigh each and every expenditure. As I sat on the sill of an open window at school one fall day, I could not help hearing a discussion between a Thomson boy and a MacArthur boy which went as follows: "You know it really costs money to go to the Alpena fair! We were down there yesterday. I wasn't there more than an hour, and zip a nickel went just like that!" That remark reminded me of the many times I had observed Mrs. Jim Thomson walking to church in the rain in order to prevent the family's new Model-T from getting wet.

Long Rapids School

Mostly, my first year of teaching was more informative than humorous. Learning about the preparation of lesson plans at County Normal had helped me as much as learning the content of the many subjects in the curriculum. World geography taught by one who had seldom been out of the county was exasperating. It was difficult to try to convince students, who had never experienced any other climate but that in Alpena county, that there were places in the world where it did not snow in the wintertime. Even I found it difficult to wax enthusiastically on the subject.

As I review that first year of teaching, I see that I was incapable of making the best use of my skills in preparing and presenting the wide range of subject matter. For example, my only introduction to teaching music had been using a pitchpipe on a few occasions in practice teaching. This did

Non-Team Teaching

not deter me from teaching the music specified in the curriculum even though Mrs. Horton next door had minored in music in her teaching preparatory work. On the other hand, she, who detested any animal that as much as wiggled, was teaching science to the third and fourth graders. My interest and self-taught techniques in the field of biology should have encouraged a trade of positions for at least a couple of classes. The end result of that mutual misuse of talents resulted in my graduating upper grade pupils who could not even hum, while Mrs. Horton turned out third and fourth graders who at an early age were oriented to killing things that moved, and would join the mass of museum goers whose interest in biology was limited to studying pickled animals in glass jars.

By and large the parents of the students were cooperative, probably out of sympathy for me. I was a victim of unpopularity on only a couple of occasions, one of which was when I took a class on a field trip, exposing them to influenza which resulted in a week's vacation for the entire school.

Methodology

In spite of the enlightened teaching philosophy I learned at County Normal, it was difficult to pry myself away from my previous school experience which was that teachers talked and students sat in straight rows and listened. The success of the learner, according to that standard, was measured by his ability to recall and write down correct answers.

It took me years to realize that as important as subject matter is, properly motivated students who are made to feel important will usually produce closer to their full potential. The emphasis in my experience thus far had not been that.

In that first year, I managed to make hard work of a profession that later proved to be stimulating and exciting. It may have been that I was too timid to stretch my luck after the field trip fiasco, but my County Normal guidance into the teaching profession kept nudging me to do a better job as a professional teacher.

Some Pupils

Even at that early age I was able to identify pupils who would probably make a place for themselves when they became adults. Allen Thomson, a younger brother of Nelson, had a mind that excelled, especially in mathematics. His ability to add, multiply, and subtract columns of figures that I would put on the chalkboard not only impressed me but often embarrassed me. Eventually I learned that it is not necessary that the teacher be the most brilliant one in the class.

My brother John, a sixth grader, was quick to comprehend and to draw others around him to share ideas and experiences. I have always felt that having me as his teacher was not the most influential experience of his life, but for me it was revealing.

I often felt that my pupils didn't learn as much as they should, but I know for sure that their teacher learned a lot of subject matter as well as techniques of class management. There were also some major drawbacks to the job. The routine of calling on each board member at the end of the month for a signature on my check was degrading. Usually, I would find each member working in a back field on his farm so the task of visiting all three consumed one Saturday a month. When I suggested that the checks be signed in advance and mailed to me on the last Friday of each month, I was told that that would make it impossible for the Board to know whether or not I had taught the required twenty days.

I volunteered that if I missed a day, I could adjust it the next month, but one board member pointed out that if I died they would have no way of correcting the records!

Knowing that one year of college was insufficient to qualify me to teach other than four grades in a two-room school, I bade farewell to each board member on my last trip to collect my salary in May of 1928. I was off to enroll in Central Michigan State Teachers College in Mt. Pleasant.

Spending the school year at the Long Rapids school, in spite of its drawbacks had its rewards. Probably the greatest one was the opportunity to get reacquainted with my family. I had been living away from home most of the year for four years, and had not been in daily contact with

RULES of the HEALTH GAME

A full bath more than once a week
Brushing teeth at least once every day
Sleeping long hours with windows open
Drinking milk but no tea or coffee
Eating some vegetables or fruit every day
Drinking at least four glasses of water every day
Playing part of every day out of doors
A bowel movement every morning
Michigan Dept. of Health,
Pearl Turner.

Board Relations

63

the problems that confronted them. Most were in the financial area and resulted from sacrifices that were made in order to keep my sister and me in high school and the County Normal in Alpena. I had some money each month, from my one hundred dollar teaching check. It was difficult to spend it on my needs, as their needs were so much greater. I was able to help here and there but I could have done much more.

*One thing they wanted was for me to describe the difference between high school and the County Normal. The same need was expressed when I returned from Central State Teachers College after spending the summer session at a **real** college. Their thirst for knowledge as well as the satisfaction that they had children in college was very real.*

CENTRAL STATE TEACHERS COLLEGE

Central Michigan State Teachers College, at Mt. Pleasant, Michigan, some one hundred and fifty miles southwest of Alpena, was the next step in my career. Having had a taste of teaching, I realized that the route to a more secure professional life was to enroll at Central and earn a Life Certificate. Doing so would allow me to complete a second year of college and be licensed to teach in rural areas for life, as long as I took an occasional refresher course at some recognized teachers' college.

I lost no time and enrolled for the summer of 1928. Whether I selected the easy courses, or my study habits had improved, I don't remember, but I received three A's that summer session.

Returning to Central in the fall, I again found myself eking out a living by stoking coal furnaces for the central heating plant and washing pots and pans at Ronan Hall, a girls' dormitory. Working at a girls' dormitory, and getting paid also, was referred to at Central as a plush job.

The College Student

It didn't take long for me to realize that the fall quarter at Central was a far cry from the six-week summer session I had attended in July. The regular students were younger and more carefree. (I was all of twenty!) Again I was being introduced to a new way of life, which I had previously experienced only to a small degree while attending Alpena County Normal.

I was impressed by the fact that even with the large enrollment, the instructors at Central seemed sincerely interested in the students as individuals. I was now a sophomore, having made up the course deficiencies that resulted from my starting at County Normal rather than in a four-year teachers college. Like my experience transferring to Alpena in high school, I had not begun at the beginning. Those who had attended their freshman year at Central had already become old hands at evaluating the courses and professors, while it was all Greek to me for several months. Within a couple of quarters though, I too was disregarding the course descriptions in the catalog and selecting my classes primarily on the reputations of the instructors.

About this time I changed the spelling of my last name. It was spelled McConnell like my father's for most of my early life. However, my birth certificate listed me as MacConnell. It would have taken court action to legalize the use of McConnell so I took the easy way out and became Mac-Connell. My brother John stayed McConnell but brother Lloyd joined me with the MacConnell appelation. Luckily Isabelle was married and didn't have to worry about the spelling of her maiden name.

The fact that Central's President Warriner was an administrator who demanded high discipline and moral standards was recognized by all seven-hundred students. His stature in the community was reinforced by the key role he played in the local Methodist Church.

My first and last encounter with the president took place in the corridor of the administration building when I saw him coming toward me wearing his black top coat over a black three piece suit, carrying his black hat in one hand and his black umbrella in the other. Of course he didn't know me from seven dollars a day. As he approached I held out my hand and said, "Good morning, Mr. President." He didn't offer his hand, but looked me straight in the eye and said, "Young man, we don't wear hats indoors here at Central." To say the least, this first encounter with a top college administrator was anything but comfortable. I quickly removed my hat and expressed my deepest regrets, no doubt very clumsily. With that, I felt for a while that my doom had been

The President

sealed at Central. The next Sunday I appeared in the front row of his Sunday School class not wearing my hat, needless to say. Perhaps this incident influenced the low priority wearing a hat has in my personal dress code.

Years later as a professor at Stanford University during the campus disturbances of the late 60's and early 70's, I couldn't help but picture President Warner confronting a Stanford student in a similar manner under those trying conditions. I think that he would have been informed in no uncertain terms what to do with his black coat and hat, and his umbrella as well.

M.L. Smith

Of all the outstanding instructors I had at Central, one, Dr. M.L. Smith, professor of Rural Education, stands out. He was an excellent teacher who bolstered and fanned the flame of my self worth. Shortly before, Dr. Smith had been awarded the first Doctor of Education degree ever given at Stanford University.

Dr. Smith was born in a sod hut in Kansas and often stated that he was born in the soil and not on it. He was for rural young people, but was against one and two-room schools. He advocated consolidated schools that offered a full 12-year program. My experience as a pupil and a teacher in those institutions immediately placed me on his wave length.

The Appleblossom Club

M.L., as Dr. Smith was known, was the extreme opposite of any other professor I had ever met. I took a half dozen

Appleblossom Club on tour

courses from him and the only difference among them was the title of the course. He sponsored a group called "The Appleblossom Club" which for the most part was made up of rural students. In that capacity he commandeered a bus from the International Harvester Company and with his various classes toured not only the rural school districts in Michigan, but other states, and Mexico and Canada as well. Short plays were written by his students and acted out for the benefit of improving education in rural areas. The theme of the plays expounded the virtues of school consolidation which we thought would attract better qualified teachers into rural areas.

Later, after becoming a teacher at Beaverton, some thirty miles away, I still maintained close ties with Dr. Smith. Eventually, bound by a common philosophy, we joined hands to help create one of the better recognized community schools in the country.

PROBLEMS AT HOME

Letters from home were a highlight, partly because my mother had a way of making light of the hardships that always seemed to plague the farm. Then in the fall of my sophomore year I received a second letter in a week's time which aroused my suspicion. My concern was confirmed when I read of the fire that had destroyed all of the farm buildings, leaving only the house standing.

The decision already had been made by my parents that I not return home, but remain in college and complete the quarter. I did go home the next weekend to see the remains of the buildings and to learn that the insurance company had decided that spontaneous combustion was the cause of the fire. Apparently my father had stored alfalfa hay in the barn before it was cured.

The fire was a disaster to my family. Although the buildings had been standing since the late 1880's, they were worth far more to us than the $1,300.00 allowed by the insurance company. My father was a broken man. He asked me to see if there were anyone at the college who could take my brother John for a while at least, since there would be no way to feed and clothe him. After a couple of days of discussions, which revealed the deep concern of our neighbors, things didn't look quite so black, and I returned to the campus to pursue my coursework.

The New Barn

Later in the year, as winter approached, a reluctant decision was made to sell the cows. Before that could be done, a light at the end of the tunnel appeared. Neighbors arrived in great numbers one day, hauling framing materials and lumber, and within a couple of days built a new red barn which was more spacious than the old one and much better organized for farm use. This wonderful gesture made me realize that although living in the country had its disadvantages, few city dwellers would be fortunate enough to experience the concern and care that neighbors had for each other in rural areas.

Although I still think that we often had more than our share of trouble, I feel a little sorry for people who breeze through life without any worries and then are completely devastated when a few obstacles appear in their paths.

GRADUATION

Graduation time finally arrived in June, 1929, and with it a valid Life Certificate based on completing two years of college. I was also completely broke. However, because of some misappropriation of teacher retirement funds in the capital, all monies paid into the plan, including mine from the one year in Long Rapids, had to be paid back. On the day before graduating I received a check for nine dollars, the most needed and appreciated check of my career to date. Again, the financial day was saved, and I had some walking around money for graduation.

Choosing Central State proved to have been a wise decision. Although there were only some seven hundred students, most of the instruction was superior and once again I had attended a school where the professors seemed to be keenly interested in the individual needs of every student. At least it was true in my case.

By mid-June I was back in Long Rapids, proud of my achievements to date but well aware of my deficiencies and the long road ahead before a bachelor's degree would become a reality. I was cognizant also of the fact that a summer job was a necessity and that with good luck a teaching position could be secured by fall.

Wheelbarrow Master

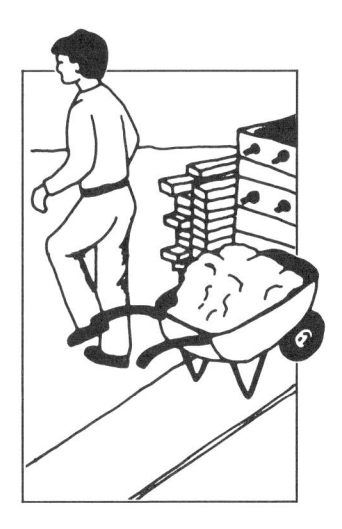

With the help of the foreman under whom I had worked at the cement plant I obtained a job pushing a wheelbarrow to dump concrete into forms for a foundry being constructed in Alpena. Mastering the technique of pushing that 200-pound mass of gray water, rock and cement, that threatened to set on a moment's notice, was difficult for my 140-pound body. On a couple of occasions the wheelbarrow and its contents slipped off the ramp resulting in my needing help to rectify the error before the arrival of the foreman. My fellow workers were quick to remind me that it would be appropriate to make use of my college education to sharpen up my wheeling technique.

As the weeks dragged on the work seemed to get harder and the prospects of getting a teaching position more remote. I thought of some of my grade-school mates who had frowned on more education because they wanted to "earn" their way through life and not sit behind a desk. I kept saying to myself that this is not my idea of a lifetime job and that there would come a day when a job would present itself that would be more to my liking.

One day in late July I received a phone call inviting me to interview for the position of science and agriculture instructor at the Beaverton Rural Agriculture School, some thirty miles northeast of Mt. Pleasant. I left the loaded wheelbarrow on the ramp. Apparently it was eventually dumped, because on my last trip to Alpena I noted that the foundry had been completed.

The benefits of a sound education were known centuries ago when Confucious said: "If your plan is for one year, plant rice; for ten years, plant trees; for 100 years, educate men."

EXCERPTS FROM BEAVERTON SCHOOL DISTRICT CONTRACTS

TEACHERS' CONTRACT

IT IS HEREBY CONTRACTED, Between the Board of Education of the **Beaverton Rural Agricultural School**, of Beaverton, Michigan, and **James MacConnell** a legally qualified teacher, that said **James MacConnell** shall teach in the Beaverton Rural Agricultural School, for the term of nine months, beginning on or about **September 11** 193**3** at a salary of **$1600.00** DOLLARS.

It is a condition of this Contract, That the holder thereof shall not accept any other position whose duties shall begin before the termination of this contract.

This Contract Shall be Void, If the holder thereof shall marry before the termination of the same (This paragraph applies to female teachers only.)

This Contract is subject to all the school laws of the State of Michigan, with which both parties agree to comply.

The Right to Transfer the holder of this contract to any building or grade is reserved by the Board; also the right to dismiss said holder of contract for inefficiency, **lack of cooperation** or immoral conduct upon thirty days notice.

It is a condition of this Contract, That if financial conditions develop whereby there would not be sufficient funds to carry on the school and pay the teachers, then upon a thirty-day notice to the holder thereof, given by the Board of Education, this contract shall be void.

This Contract may be Terminated upon thirty days notice by either party to this contract.

Dated this **8** day of **September** A. D. 193**3**

Signed *James MacConnell*

Board of Education, Beaverton Rural Agricultural School

1933—Note addition of "lack of cooperation" clause to cause for dismissal. Also contract voided by marriage (female only!).

1930—Notice of Hiring.

Office of Board of Education, School Dist. No. 1, Frl.

Beaverton, Mich., *April 23* 1930

To *James MacConnell*

You are hereby notified that you have been appointed by the Board of Education of School District No. 1 frl.., Beaverton, Michigan, as a teacher in the public schools for the ensuing school year, as hereinafter provided:

School *Beaverton* Position *Agriculture*
Grade *12 months* Salary *1800.00*

The right to transfer you to any other building, or grade is reserved by the board, and the board can dismiss you at any time for inefficiency or immoral conduct.

If you desire to accept the position, please sign the form of acceptance on the back of this card and return to the Superintendent within ten days from date hereof.

Arthur E. D___ *Maude B. Higgeman*
(Over) President. Secretary.

Beaverton, Michigan, April 26, 1933

Mr. MacConnell,

At a special meeting held April 25, 1933 the Board of Education voted to offer you a contract for the coming year. It is impossible at this time to say definitely what the salary will be but we think you can depend on the Board being fair to the teachers in this matter.

Maude B. Higgeman
Secretary

1933—Letter of appointment during Depression when school funds unknown.

1936 Superintendent contract. Note incentive pay for bring in Tobacco Township.

James David MacConnell, a legally qualified teacher in the State of Michigan, that the said **James David MacConnell**, shall teach in the said district for a term of **nine** months beginning **September 1**, 1936. The said teacher to work in the following departments **Superintendent**

The Board of Education has the priviledge to shift the said teacher to any grade or building.

The said district agrees to pay said **James David MacConnell** the sum of **$2,600.00 providing no new territory is added, and the sum of $2,800.00 providing Tobacco Township joins with this district.** Dollars. This contract shall hold for a period of two years.

Professional Growth in Beaverton

The second employment interview of my life was successful and when school started a few days later I was a high school teacher. Teaching at Beaverton proved to be much different from teaching the upper grades at Long Rapids, and the additional college experience definitely increased my confidence as a teacher. The faculty was small and the high school program was conducted in the upper four rooms of the school as well as in two rooms in the basement. I did most of my teaching in agriculture, biology and general science in a basement classroom across from the boys' toilet and adjacent to the general shop which was shared with the chemistry teacher. I did teach United States Government in a more prestigious room on the second floor. Not having much interest or training in government, I always felt more at home in the basement, despite the smell of formaldehyde and a variety of other odors.

The school district had recently been consolidated, taking in seven elementary schools in Beaverton township that bordered the village. The election that closed the one-room schools generated many conflicts and polarized those living in the township. Much of my time during the first two years was devoted to community relations. As I made my rounds of the district contacting parents and students who were participating in projects of the 4-H Club and its high school counterpart, the Future Farmers of America, I acted as a catalyst for our superintendent, Mr. Ralph Shepard.

The need for change was evident. For example, rural high school students were denied the opportunity to participate in sports because they had to leave for home on the buses at four o'clock and could not stay for practice. This was later rectified by scheduling a second bus trip to take the rural

> **Heads Beaverton Farmers' Group**
>
> Mr. MacConnell, advisor of the Future Farmers of America Chapter of Beaverton and five boys of the Beaverton Chapter will soon be on their return from Washington, D. C., where they have had three great days' experience at the nation's capital with other Future Farmer boys from other states.
>
> Mr. MacConnell was accompanied by Victor Schember, state farmer and local president of the Beaverton chapter, Franklin Niggeman, third place speaker in the State F. F. A. speaking contest, Elwood Barberree, Chapter Reporter, Willis McCulloch, State Farmer and candidate for American Farmer degree, Louis Hall, editor of the Beaverton F. F. A. paper.

The Catalyst

athletes home at a later hour. We also tried to make the school part of the township affairs by assigning teachers to attend rural social functions such as chicken dinners which were common then.

June Ross

One of the requisites of a satisfactory life is meeting and enjoying new acquaintances. June Oliver (later Ross) and her mother lived in a small three-bedroom Aladdin-built house two blocks from the school. They took the principal, Ralph Van Vulkenberg, and me into their home and provided board and room for only seven dollars per week. They were thoughtful and kind people and we always looked forward to returning to their home after a full day, and often evening, at school. On a recent trip to Beaverton we had a great visit with June who was looking forward to her 94th birthday.

At the beginning of my second year at Beaverton I met and married Christine Cahow, one of the best teachers in the system. We rented a small house for $25.00 per month, borrowed against our insurance policies to buy a refrigerator and a stove, and set up housekeeping. When the landlord raised the rent to $30.00 per month, we moved out and bought a three-bedroom house for $3,000.00. The fact that the house was adjacent to the school had both advantages and disadvantages, but at least we were not paying exhorbitant rent.

OFF TO MICHIGAN STATE

After my second year of teaching in Beaverton and with a lot of work by a lot of people, word was getting around that Beaverton was becoming a successful community school.

Probably because of the growing reputation of the school, I was visited by Mr. E.E. Gallup, State Director of Vocational Education, who proved to be another key person in my life. He encouraged me to seek a leave of absence for a year, attend Michigan State College, and earn a bachelor's degree and a Smith-Hughes diploma. The latter would qualify the school district for Federal funds. The prospect of Federal funds whetted the Board's appetite and hardly before I knew it I was off to Michigan State on a half-time salary which at that time came to nine hundred dollars. Fortunately, during the first two years at Beaverton I had taken evening and Saturday classes at Central and was within a year of earning my Bachelor of Arts degree.

Class Size

Up to then most of my educational experience had been at a college of some seven-hundred students. Now I was in one of four thousand students. Classes no longer numbered twenty or thirty students, but three or four hundred. Attention to individuals was minimal. Instructors walked into the classrooms, mounted the elevated dais, made their pitch and walked out. Some of the presentations were not of the highest quality. A teacher talking to the chalkboard with his back to the class was a common occurrence.

The smaller specialized classes resembled those at Central, which was heartening to me, as was the School of Education itself, where again the professors gave sound teaching techniques a high priority.

Although Michigan State was not a teachers college, its College of Education was one of the best in the Midwest. The education courses were interesting and informative. The objective of all Michigan State's practice teaching courses was to prepare students to teach agriculture, and each student was given the opportunity to show his creativity in this area. My practice teaching was under the direction of a Mr. Smith, who lived and breathed vocational education. I remember that he signed his letters, "Vocationally yours".

In preparing for one of my demonstration lessons with a seventh grade class I brought in two armadillos to demonstrate that protective coats were not confined to turtles. The next morning Mr. Smith was greeted by a three-legged desk, a substantial hole in the corner of the door leading to his room, and my prize armored exhibits lodged behind an upright steam radiator. His succinct statement was that from now on I should be cognizant of the fact that animals with sharp teeth often seek freedom.

As time passed and my students sometimes did things that didn't make sense, the sharing of that incident usually was a good substitute for a reprimand.

BACK TO CENTRAL STATE

After spending two quarters at Michigan State, I was advised by Mr. Gallup to return to Central Michigan State College and take my degree there in the spring of 1932. He said he would then recommend me to be superintendent of schools at Beaverton, for there were rumors that a vacancy was going to occur. Before I left, he invited me to spend a night at his home and took me to the Hotel Olds in Lansing for dinner. After that evening I realized that he was truly interested in my being a successful educator as well as a careful manager of time. In assuring me that I would be appointed to the Beaverton superintendency, he recommended that I stay there no longer than six or seven years and to try and arrange my time so as to never take another full-time job again. His enlightened philosophy was, "Never sell all of your time to any one person or agency but save at least twenty percent for reading, investing and a little day dreaming."

Rationale

Leaving Michigan State after two terms and graduating from Central precluded my receiving a Smith Hughes Certificate. That would have taken another year of study and my leave of absence from Beaverton was only for two terms. This decision made sense to both Mr. Gallup and me, as vocational agriculture teachers were still in short supply and I was needed at Beaverton. We felt that if I could weather the storm as a superintendent of schools for a while I could then employ an agriculture teacher. The job would introduce me to the field of school administration which was high on my education priority list.

THE YOUNGEST SUPERINTENDENT

Everything happened as Mr. Gallup had predicted and in the fall of 1932 I became the youngest superintendent of schools in Michigan. The school system had an enrollment of around four hundred. I was much too young and inexperienced to assume the responsibilities of the community's educational leader, but I got the job, and was later awarded a contract that provided for a salary escalation if I were successful in persuading other townships and one-room schools to join the Beaverton school district.

For the next three years I had a twelve-month job as superintendent of schools and agriculture teacher, which resulted in substantial savings to the district.

Being superintendent at my age was a learning experience for me and for the community. I didn't know enough to be superintendent, but I did know rural people and my contacts as agriculture teacher were helpful.

During the first year on the job, my hair started to turn gray—and not from cement dust this time. Some of the challenging people and events I had to deal with as superintendent were no doubt responsible. Later in my career at Stanford my colleague, Professor William Odell, who had been Superintendent of Schools of Oakland, California, often spoke of his administrative cabinet which he used in his decision making process. At Beaverton I was my own cabinet in charge of fire fighting. Seldom did a day pass that didn't provide an opportunity for someone in the school district to become an active participant in a crisis. Problems of bus scheduling, curriculum changes, faculty misunderstandings, custodial discontent and many more always ended up on my desk.

The position of superintendent of a small school district carried with it many of the same duties and responsibilities as those in larger cities, such as Bay City, Saginaw, Flint and others within a radius of one hundred miles of Beaverton.

Although the titles were the same, when the day came for me to represent our school system in a joint educational meeting sponsored by Benjamin Klager, Superintendent of the Bay City Schools, I was most uncomfortable. I practiced

HEADS SCHOOL AT BEAVERTON

"Jim" MacConnell New Superintendent

James MacConnell, agriculture teacher, will be superintendent of the Beaverton Agricultural School next year. His appointment by the school board was confirmed Friday by E. E. Gallup, state supervisor of vocational education.

MacConnell will replace Perry R. Hoover, present superintendent. He will also continue in his former capacity as agriculture teacher. The consolidation of the two positions became necessary when the school board was faced with the necessity of trimming the budget for the next year.

In his position as agriculture teacher MacConnell has won considerable fame throughout the state through the Future Farmer organization which he has sponsored. Last fall the Beaverton chapter of this national group was awarded the plaque for being the best all-around group in Michigan. There are over 100 chapters in the state.

Ben Klager

my speech for the meeting and also my handshake and introductory remarks. Ben Klager was a huge man with hands like hams. As he offered his hand and towered over me, I forgot my prepared remarks and stumbled to my seat that was one of some fifteen that encircled the largest conference table I had ever seen.

I remember little that took place at the meeting, but I shall never forget the giant hand and the huge frame and kind face of the man who extended it to me.

Why Me?   Being appointed superintendent was credited by some to my brilliance, while others thought that luck had played the key role. The truth was that although I was not totally qualified, and was certainly shy on experience, I was there and as well suited for the job as anyone else available. It really wasn't that great a position. I also suspected that in the future I would be credited with having had superintendency experience and that there would be few questions as to the size of the school district.

Later, when I was hard pressed by outsiders for a truthful reason for my appointment, I would tell people that I had gone to this little community seeking a teaching job. I had made contact with the president of the board who questioned me about my areas of specialization only to discover that each teaching position for which I was qualified had been filled or was not being offered. At that point I would tell my listeners that I snapped my fingers and said disgustedly, "Well, I'm a son of a bitch." Immediately the Board president responded, "Well, why didn't you say so in the first place? We're looking for a superintendent for our school!"

The lot of a superintendent of schools is not easy these days with the harassment of financial problems and litigious parents, pupils and teachers. But it was equally trying at our level of experience in the newly consolidated district.

As superintendent, the need to delegate responsibilities was probably the most difficult technique that I had to learn. Recognizing that there are others who can perform tasks and thus multiply one's own efforts is a must.

JDM, circa 1932

The Good Shepherd

This was brought home to me dramatically one evening when I escorted a teacher to a neighboring community to visit her sister on a family problem. While returning ground fog had settled in the low spots. One apparent fog area turned out to be a flock of sheep which resulted in a mutton massacre. Twenty-five sheep were killed or maimed and I appeared on the streets of Beaverton the next morning with the only automobile in town with a fur lined chassis and wool wheels.

The lawsuits that resulted between the owner, myself and the insurance company did little to enhance my position with the farmers in the school district. The complications would have been lessened had the farmer not pushed for a bonus on each sheep, for he claimed that those leading the flock were his best sheep and that he should be paid an additional ten dollars each to compensate him for his losses.

As I was arranging for the hearings and trial I decided once and for all that it was wiser to employ others to perform auxiliary duties and save my time for duties that were more closely related to my profession.

Miss Mae Shell

Miss Shell was an eighth grade teacher who was known as a disciplinarian. She was close to six feet tall and was notorious for ruling by fear. It was common knowledge that her class, while standing at attention, breathed in unison. She would usually clear up any potential discipline problems shortly after the first student made a move to see how far either he or she could go. Physical encounter would take place on the spot and the winner was invariably Miss Shell. After a basketball game one night when we lost to Gladwin High School, she came up to me, shook her finger in my face and said, ''Mr. MacConnell you should be ashamed! If I couldn't beat them, I wouldn't play them!''

Action

The third month of school Miss Shell grabbed a misbehaving girl in the corridor and in the scuffle tore part of her dress off. Even though she had always been referred

Miss Mae Schell on right

Reaction

to as their best teacher when they were in school, the parents felt she had at last discredited her usefulness and now must go. A petition demanding her resignation landed on my desk with the signatures of at least ninety percent of the people in the district. Soon a meeting of the Board was scheduled in the old study hall and a packed house was present. The chairman, Mr. Dann, asked if there were any "partitions" to be presented. One of the parents of the girl stood up and read the petition. Before the board was to vote, however, Miss Shell rose to her feet and proceeded to call each parent by name and to identify his or her weaknesses as a student some twenty-five years earlier. She reminded all present that any success they had had to date was no doubt because of her good teaching and not because they were good students. Had she at that point said, "Come to the blackboard and diagram the following sentence," I am certain that there would have been a number of parents trampled to death attempting to be number one at the board.

I sat beside the president and wondered why my school administration books had not outlined the course of procedure to follow next. Finally, Mr. Dann stood and said, "Meeting dismissed!" The formerly irate parents marched out row by row, and the next morning Miss Shell was back parsing sentences and the parents were at home caring for their many duties just as Miss Shell thought should be their roles.

As I worked with Miss Shell over the next few years I learned to love and respect her for her ability to govern as well as earn the respect of the community. Stories of her disciplinary activities continued to make the rounds, especially the first week of each school year when she selected her first victim. I always admired her honesty and loyalty to me and to the community, even though she made me a little nervous in that I never knew what her next move would be. In summarizing my recollections of Miss Shell, I have mixed feelings about her as a teacher—something like the husband who watched his mother-in-law drive his new Cadillac over a cliff. As a friend and as my pilot in troubled waters, she always held a high priority position in my life.

78

Miss Schwitzer

The next year, a near riot was sparked by a sixth grade teacher, Miss Schwitzer, who dispensed with saluting the flag one day because of a late bus. Many thought that the name, Schwitzer, was a dead giveaway that she was pro-German and sympathetic toward the Nazis who had taken power in Germany. Putting out the fires of contention twenty miles away from the school on occasions like that proved to be a full time job for me, and every diplomatic maneuver in the book had to be used to restore the confidence of the community in the school and its staff.

ACCREDITATION

Then came a visit from the North Central Association—the accrediting agency for schools and colleges in that area. Although the inspector was not much older than I, he appeared to have access to a more stable funding source than did the school district that he was inspecting. After spending the day making observations that did not meet his high educational standards, he stopped by my office for a one-way interview. He informed me that our school had about as inadequate a curriculum and as poor a quality of teaching as he had ever witnessed.

He said that we probably were not going to be accredited. He cited teacher morale, inadequate supplies, discipline problems, and even the condition of the building that had been standing there with a minimum of repairs since 1908.

Let's Trade

I had to make some kind of dramatic move in order to save the school from disaster and to protect my own neck from being stretched beyond its limit. So I stepped from behind my desk and invited him to take my seat as Superintendent of Beaverton Schools. After doing so it took but a minute to point out that the local bank had closed two months earlier and that the teachers were not being paid.

The next move was to show him a newspaper article that announced that the Gladwin Bank at the county seat eight miles north of us had also closed, impounding tax funds that had been deposited there for the purpose of paying teachers. I looked him in the eye and asked what I felt was a fair question. "Now you are the Superintendent of the Beaverton schools. What would you do?" He answered by admitting that he didn't believe that he could improve on the situation. When we traded seats again, he stated that he was going to accredit our high school for another two years, trusting that by the end of that period conditions would improve and I would then be able to upgrade the system.

INSUBORDINATION

The policy of the Board was to evaluate teachers in early December and accept recommendations for new staff members when vacancies occured. At one meeting Mr. Dann, the president of the Board, notified all present that he had hired his daughter to fill a fourth grade vacancy. Having learned in my school administration courses that board members were policy makers and that only administration should recommend personnel, I objected. I made it clear that I had nothing against Miss Dann, but that after reviewing other eligible candidates I would make the decision on which candidate to recommend.

That meeting turned out to be a memorable one. Shortly before midnight I was asked to leave the meeting so the Board could vote on whether or not to cancel my contract because of insubordination. After the vote I was notified that I was to continue as superintendent, but I learned later that although there were three members who felt I should remain, there was another member who had voted with the president.

By early spring the school board once again was acting more like a board according to the textbooks on school administration, and I had been reinstated in my role as educational leader of the community.

Old patterns were changing. Mr. Dann, the Board Chairman had not been a recognized community leader. Politically he was a Democrat and there had long been agreement in Beaverton that Democrats had about the same degree of influence in the community as Catholics did in Long Rapids.

SCHOOL HIRES NEW TEACHERS

Plans for the opening of the Beaverton Consolidated School this Fall were announced today by Supt. James MacConnell. The school term will begin on Tuesday, September 4. Miss Val Rae Cutcher, Life certificate, Michigan State Normal College, will teach first grade. Miss Cutcher was hired by the Rural Agricultural School Board Tuesday evening. Miss Niggeman, Life C. S. T. C., will continue as second-grade teacher; Miss Ruth Pobanz, Life C. S. T. C., will teach the third and part of the fourth grade; Miss Janet Dann, A. B., C. S. T. C., will teach the remainder of the fourth and part of the fifth grade. Mrs. Grover Babcock will be in charge of the sixth and part of the seventh grade. Miss Mae Shell will share part of the seventh and teach the eigth grade.

However, now that Franklin D. Roosevelt was President of the United States, Democrats were not to be brushed aside. In addition to his duties as the printer of the Beaverton Clarion, Mr. Dann had been appointed postmaster.

Having been watching from the sidelines for so long, Mr. Dann was not adequately prepared for his community leadership role. This was especially true in the field of public speaking. When he realized that he was to pass out the high school diplomas at graduation, and to deliver a short speech as well, he told me that he would greatly appreciate it if I would write the speech. Unfortunately, I was as inadequately prepared as he was to prepare that speech but was willing to try, and decided to make it an historical presentation. My final draft started out, "One thousand years ago, this was a howling wilderness," and I went on from there. At the designated time in the graduation ceremony Mr. Dann stepped up to the podium with a pale face and trembling hands and spoke as follows: "One thousand years ago this was a howling wilderness." Then his face turned a pale green color as he once again tried to read the prepared script and repeated, "One thousand years ago this was a howling wilderness." His third and last attempt went, "A thousand years ago this was a howling wilderness and I wish to Hell it was yet. Come up and get your diplomas!"

Community Pride

Each year the Beaverton district's reputation as a community school grew until it became a beacon among schools of its type in the Midwest—to the reflected glory of many of its patrons. One day Mrs. Budge, wife of a highly respected leader in the community, was being questioned by a potential buyer for the family drug store. After awaiting a let-up in her recital of the merits of the school, he said, "Mrs. Budge, I came here to buy your drugstore, not your school."

Ida McGuire, A Natural Leader

The need for administrators to be educational leaders was constantly brought to my attention. One of my first moves on becoming a full-time superintendent was to employ Mrs. Ida McGuire as grade school principal. She had a small daughter, had been divorced and her parents were farmers in the district—all negatives in those days.

Mrs. McGuire accepted the position knowing that the cards were stacked against her. As it turned out she was a natural leader and teacher—not only of children, but of teachers as well.

Within a couple years of her appointment the Beaverton grade school was becoming known for its teaching techniques and improved pupil learning results. She was able to implement some of the then radical educational ideas we jointly developed. Team teaching, field trips, individualized instruction and community participation became part of the new curriculum.

ANNEXATION

We had been successful in attracting additional townships and one-room schools to join the Beaverton District. One holdout, the Buckeye District, with about twenty students and an assessed valuation of only fifty-thousand dollars, had come to the end of the road in its ability to finance itself. Since Beaverton was adjacent and was already caring for Buckeye's secondary students, it seemed appropriate for Buckeye to be annexed as an additional member of Beaverton's growing family.

I consulted the attorney who represented all governmental agencies in the county and was advised that a Monday was as good a day as any for an annexation election as long as sufficient time was allowed to properly notify the citizenry. So, notices were sent out, the election held, and sufficient favorable votes cast to approve the annexation.

Legally, ten days were required after the vote before the final annexation documents were completed. Within that period of time, an event occurred to again jeopardize my position as superintendent of schools. The event was the successful drilling of an oil well in the Buckeye district. Visions of opulence suddenly took over. The Township Board, the agency responsible for completing the annexation, notified me that because of the district's new found wealth, it would not carry out the mandate of the voters. Instead, Buckeye now planned to build its own high school, and perhaps a college.

I went to the county attorney and was told that the Beaverton Board should mandate that the annexation had been completed, and as the school board's representative, I could sign the necessary papers. This I did and then committed a major error. I authorized the County Sheriff to round up the Township Board members and lock them in the county jail for not carrying out the wishes of the district voters.

The Lawsuit

A lawsuit followed and I found our board members who previously had backed me were impartially scattered among other observers in the audience at the trial. The Township Board's attorneys accused me of deliberately setting the date of the election on Labor Day, a holiday when a number of taxpayers left the district on trips that had been previously planned.

I was accused further of directing teachers to post election notices on the backs of telephone poles where they could not be seen. To make matters even worse, my notes on the agreement with the district to transfer the school desks and other equipment were written on small pieces of paper. The accusers presented their documents neatly typed on legal-sized paper with red lines separating the margins from the body of the text. The teachers involved as helpers, were summoned to appear and subject themselves to questioning.

Each day, on returning to court after a sleepless night, seemed to be darker than the previous one. I carefully watched Judge Shaffer, who up until then I had felt was a friend of mine. I could not guess what his ruling would be. I knew that I had done nothing dishonest, and that I was being accused of doing things that were indeed farfetched. But I didn't know what was going on in Judge Shaffer's mind.

The Verdict

However, I had made up my mind that as discouraged as I was, I would see it to the end as gracefully as I could. Since I had no choice, that appeared to be a sound decision. Finally, on the fifth day, the Judge rapped his gavel, declared that he was ordering the Buckeye Township Board to turn the school district over to the Beaverton School District as the voters had decreed, and walked out of the courtroom.

This proved to be a fortunate decision. It probably saved my job, as well as the life of the Buckeye district since it takes a lot of oil at three dollars a barrel to build and maintain a high school, let alone a college.

I was amazed at how many friends I had the next day, and how often at the next board meeting I was complimented on the way I had handled this most unfortunate situation.

Several weeks after the decision I asked Judge Shaffer why he ruled the way he did. His answer was, "Jim, take a look at the new county jail that was built with the proceeds from oil. It is filled with people who talk too much. Those attorneys were talking too much and I was tired, so I ruled in your favor."

PROBLEMS WITH BUSSING

After the lawsuit and other experiences with the law and its quirks, I became a believer in acquainting students of school administration with the pitfalls to avoid in areas where the law can become involved. One such area is school bussing. Bussing was usually a controversial topic in rural communities when patrons had to decide whether or not to give up their one- and two-room schools and transport their children to nearby centers. Any incident on the bus became a major tragedy regardless of its real importance.

Superintendent Kennie Bordine experienced that kind of controversy at Marlette, Michigan. While conducting a meeting on bussing, a mother asked what would happen if her boy had to go to the bathroom enroute to or from school. Kennie's answer was, "If he has to go, he has to go. We would stop the bus and let him go." The patrons of the Beaverton district were no exception.

Bus Drivers

School bus drivers have a responsibility that is seldom recognized, but is always publicized when even a small accident occurs. We tried to recognize the contributions of the Beaverton drivers by providing sharp looking uniforms to add a dimension of pride in the position. Safety courses were conducted to keep them constantly reminded of their responsibilities as trusted school district employees.

When the Beaverton district first purchased five 28-passenger Chevrolet buses, it was emphasized that the buses were an asset, not a hazard, to the community. Extra runs were made to make it possible for rural children to participate in athletics.

The first generation Chevrolet buses proved to be faithful servants during the early years of the unified school district. Advertising the hazardous condition of roads over which school children were being transported in those small buses embarrassed the county road commissioner and influenced him to blacktop the roads throughout the southern part of Gladwin County.

Promoting Good Will

As a good will gesture, I had encouraged the use of school buses for 4-H and other auxilliary activities. Trips to Farmers Week at Michigan State College as well as to Future Farmers of America gatherings became fairly routine. One embarrassing situation resulted from my scheduling a two-day trip to East Lansing for thirty Future Farmer members and arriving a week late. A Watergate style cover-up could not be employed so I admitted guilt, and suffered the humiliation.

The trips were not looked upon by the School Board with much enthusiasm, and their skipticism proved justified on one occasion when County Agriculture Agent Jesse Huggett asked to use a bus to transport 4-H Club members on an outing some forthy miles away. Wheel spindles on buses have been known to crystalize and break, resulting in a detached wheel. This is exactly what happened on the 4-H trip as a slow curve was being negotiated. The left wheel preceded the bus by a couple of hundred feet and did severe damage to a Plymouth being driven by an elderly man.

Although the school district was adequately covered with insurance for all possible situations, the insurance company maintained that the bus did not cause the accident, but that the wheel was the culprit. Since there were no injuries and a major claim could not have resulted, a decision was made to repair the Plymouth and a potential lawsuit avoided.

I was on the opposite side of the fence once when returning from a student trip to Niagara Falls. We had stopped in Monroe, Michigan for breakfast and after driving a half hour beyond Monroe I noted the students passing around ash trays, salt and pepper shakers, and eating utensils. We pulled to the shoulder of the road and a lively discussion ensued. Within minutes we agreed that the items had been taken from the restaurant and that they had to be returned, although not with total unanimity. Whether or not the trip back and confronting the restaurant owner had any lasting effects on the students, I do not know. But one thing I have always been fairly certain about is that many uncomfortable situations can result from ill-gotten gains.

THE NEW BUSES

The introduction of larger buses to the school district was a memorable occasion. Selecting the units to be purchased was a major decision on the part of the Board. It finally decided that the new carriers were to be International trucks with Wayne bodies. We planned to pick them up and drive them home from the body factory in Wayne, Indiana.

The meeting regarding the delivery should have been routine. Obviously, the head bus driver and four additional drivers would go to Wayne and drive the five buses home. But a hidden agenda emerged as one of the board members, Bill Grant, announced that he was going to drive one of the buses himself. This not only was highly irregular, but since Bill had driven nothing larger than a Model-A Ford, it was even dangerous. The head driver, Jim Isanlower, and I discussed the matter and decided that excessive insurance was indicated. I drove the drivers to Wayne and was impressed that those big buses looked even bigger as we inspected them and proudly noted the name, Beaverton Rural Agricultural School, painted on the side of each.

In The Rear

After deciding that board member Grant should bring up the rear, where he would have less chance of causing an accident, we set out for home. At the Michigan state line I moved ahead of the caravan in order to get home and have time to alert the townspeople to meet the caravan in a couple of hours should anyone so desire.

On arriving home my worst fears were justified. I answered the phone to learn that while watching some ditch diggers without realizing that the number one bus had stopped, Bill had plowed into the fourth bus, seriously incapacitating both buses. The heavy insurance proved to be a sound idea. The accident was upsetting to morale in the district and I looked forward with trepidation to the next board meeting. The subject was not mentioned!

Since childhood I had felt that rural people did not have an equal break with those born in the cities. This observation was verified when I stood by two women at the Alpena County fair and heard one of them remark as a farmer and his family drove up in their Model-T, "Even farmers have automobiles today!"

At the beginning of one fall term, I had an opportunity to demonstrate my dedication to those feelings. School had been in session only a couple of days when an elderly black man with a white beard, sitting in a buggy with a beautiful black woman and a teen-age girl, stopped in front of my office. I watched as a short conversation took place between the old man and the younger woman. Then hesitantly, the mother and child dismounted and slowly walked to the door and into my office. The mother was charming. She introduced herself as Mrs. Holly and presented the child, whose looks were not enhanced by her large welfare glasses.

Mrs. Holly's simple statement was, "They wouldn't let Elizabeth get on the bus." I knew of course that there were not more than a half dozen black people in the Beaverton service area, and that they were located along the Gladwin-Midland County line. Those residing on the Midland side were outside of the school district, while those living across the road on the Gladwin County side were residents of

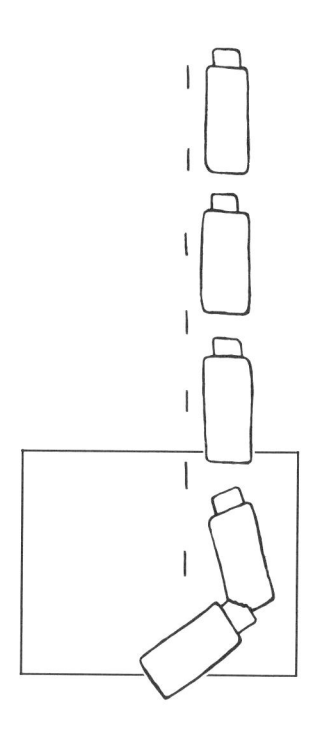

Elizabeth, The Holly That Bloomed

87

Beaverton Township and within the boundaries of the Beaverton School District. Elizabeth was from the wrong side of the road, and therefore not eligible to ride on the bus and attend our high school.

After carefully explaining this unfortunate technical situation to Mrs. Holly, I said that I would try to arrange it so that Elizabeth could ride the bus and come to our high school. Little did I know that I was paving the way for a very serious confrontation with the red tape of bureaucracy.

As it happened, the board was meeting that night, so I presented what I felt was a routine request. Would we be breaking the law by allowing Elizabeth to ride the bus? Who would pay the seventy-five dollars for yearly tuition? These were among the many questions discussed. Finally, I suggested that I contact the State Department of Education in Lansing, to clear the legal roadblocks, if any existed, for Elizabeth to attend Beaverton High School.

Bureaucratic Red Tape

To my surprise and disgust I was informed by the state that Elizabeth would have to go to high school in Midland, Michigan, some ten miles from her home, although no transportation was provided. Even worse, since the one-room school that she had attended was not a part of the Midland district, she would be required to pay tuition.

My next move was to call a special board meeting that nearly proved to be my undoing. I suggested that we break the law, absorb the tuition and allow Elizabeth to ride the bus. I was confident that justice would prevail, so I put my job on the line and stated that either Elizabeth should be allowed to attend school in Beaverton, or that the Board could get a new superintendent. At 2:00 AM the next morning Elizabeth's admission was part of the minutes of the special meeting.

I am proud to say that Elizabeth graduated as valedictorian of her class and went on to the Freedmen's School of Nursing affiliated with Howard University in Washington, D.C. where she was later head nurse. She held nursing jobs in large New York City hospitals and was the first black nurse hired at Good Samaritan Hospital on Long Island and received service awards from the A.M.A. Now a widow, she has three sons, a physician, a nurse, and a teacher. I grieve about the number of promising young people like Elizabeth Holly who have never been given the opportunity to bloom.

SCHOOL PLANNING

The need for a new high school soon became apparent and I helped the Board qualify for a federal matching grant to construct the new school. This precipitated much community involvement and was my first experience with school planning—a step towards my eventual life's work.

REFORESTATION

We were successful in pursuading the state to sell the district 40 acres and later 120 acres of scab land for one dollar to be reforested by school children. Skeptics criticized the project, especially when additional WPA funds were given to fence the first forty acre tract that was within a mile and a half of the new school. Some said that the Lord had failed to make trees grow on that land so MacConnell decided to try. Norway and white pines were planted in plowed furrows. The seedlings were so small that one hundred trees could be held in one hand. Although some bunches of one hundred ended up under a log, the first two summers proved to be wet, and the resultant school-owned forest prospered and has been commercially harvested on two occasions.

FAREWELL TO BEAVERTON

Three years after I became superintendent in Beaverton, it was clear that the dual jobs of superintendent and vocational agriculture teacher were unwieldy, so a full-time agriculture teacher was employed. This freed me to pursue graduate work at the University of Michigan during the summer months. In the summer of 1940, I completed my Master's Degree in School Administration there under the direction of Dr. Arthur B. Moehlman.

The contacts made at the University of Michigan over the years proved fruitful for just a few days before Christmas, 1940, I received a telephone call from Dr. Howard McClusky,

Vice President of the University and a Professor of Education asking me if I were going to stay in Beaverton all of my life or did I want to come to the University on a scholarship and work toward my Doctor's degree? I asked him how much the position would pay and his answer was, "More than you are getting now." Although ultimately I found that the facts weren't quite as he optimistically had painted them, I did call the president of the Beaverton School Board and resign that afternoon.

THOSE WONDERFUL YEARS

As I look back on my experience in Beaverton, it is clear that I certainly was not the best superintendent in the state, but what I lacked in training and experience, I made up for in enthusiasm. Beaverton was becoming recognized as a community school interested in serving the town and rural children and anyone else who was interested in benefitting from what the district had to offer. Later in life, I had many responsibilities and positions of honor, but I always regard my years at Beaverton as among the best I ever experienced.

There were many outstanding people with whom I came in contact during those Beaverton years. Two were Harry and Ruth Goldberg, owners of Goldberg's Mercantile store in Gladwin, the county seat. They were supportive of my ambitions and early on Harry encouraged me to invest a part of my modest salary and even do a bit of speculating. He felt that being a young man I would have time to recover if an investment turned sour.

Great Students

It may be trite to say, but each of the Beaverton students was unique. Each had one or more talents, an intellectual, a mechanical or a social intelligence that could be nurtured or an internal drive or work ethic that made him or her a contributing member of society when entering the "world" after leaving the Beaverton schools. I am proud to have had a small part to play in getting them started on the road to success. Among the students there were many who were outstanding then and continued to be so in their later careers.

Two of the many come to mind: Victor Schember and Alfred Asch. Victor was one of our FFA boys who went on to Michigan State College and ended up as a professor in the field of agriculture at Texas A&M College. Alfred delayed going to college, but when he did he took off, literally and figuratively. He was commissioned in the Army Air Corps and served as a bomber pilot in World War II. After his bemedalled flying career he became involved with introducing computer applications to the U.S. Air Force and the U.S. Defense Intelligence Agency in Washington, D.C. Subsequent to his retirement as a full colonel he continued work in computer applications as a civilian with a Washington, D.C. company. Now he has retired again. He sparked the petition drive that resulted in the special commendation appearing on page 92 for which I am grateful to him and all the others who participated.

> Among the many facts I learned in Beaverton was that people would forgive your mistakes if they knew that you were honest and sincere. I also learned that as much as some people would try to work you into a position of community conflict, they all could be influenced by the human touch. Offering to transport the mourners at a funeral would always pay dividends and the closer the superintendent's automobile was to the hearse the better. In other words, the key to maintaining popularity correlates highly with common sense.

The AASA

The Beaverton superintendency helped me grow personally and also taught me the importance of growing professionally. Although money was a scarce commodity I had managed to save enough to join the American Association of School Administrators and to attend its national convention in Cleveland, Ohio in 1935. There I was introduced to the art of speaking in public as I observed national educational leaders on the platform who up to that time had been only names in a book to me. In spite of the interruptions that came along, I continued to be an active member of AASA and received some recognition on a couple of occasions as an emeritus member.

Who says your past doesn't catch up with you?

STATE OF MICHIGAN

SPECIAL TRIBUTE

DR. JAMES D. MacCONNELL

LET IT BE KNOWN, That we are extremely honored to recognize Dr. James D. MacConnell for his untiring and imaginative efforts during the depression years of the 1930s and in the ensuing years to accomplish major improvements in the educational system at Beaverton, Michigan, and the surrounding rural areas. Through his leadership, the Beaverton School was established as one of the early "rural agricultural high schools" in Michigan. This oriented the school more in keeping with the essentially farm-based nature of the community.

As one of the youngest superintendents in the state, Dr. MacConnell brought recognition to Beaverton and the local community in coalescing educational interests among several townships. The busing of students to the central schools at all grade levels eliminated the one-room country schools and gave opportunity for a much larger segment of youths to obtain a secondary degree. The outstanding success of the consolidation program greatly improved education, giving students more options for college selection, and it served as a model for other districts within and outside the state to implement similar programs.

To accommodate the increase in the student population at the central school, Dr. MacConnell acquired classroom space at a church and had country school buildings moved to the city. Following this, he obtained funds through federal government programs to build a new, modern high school.

Due to Dr. MacConnell's foresight and good judgment, the Future Farmers of America (FFA) were organized. FFA projects and other projects taught students about conservation and long-term planning. Such a project was the acquisition of forty acres of relatively poor land from the state for $1.00 for the Beaverton School District. This land was cleared and planted in the early 1930s with Norway and white pine seedlings furnished by the state, with the work accomplished through FFA student projects and volunteer labor. The land was fenced in through the use of federal funds. The project had outstanding success as the trees are now ready for harvest for high grade lumber which will provide needed revenue to the school district. This project, the first of its kind by the school district, served as a model for efficient land use and it demonstrated what can be accomplished with limited resources through imagination, cooperation, and leadership. Clearly, Dr. MacConnell's activity in the field of education will have a lasting impact on life in Beaverton for many years to come.

IN SPECIAL TRIBUTE, Therefore, This document is signed and presented to Dr. James D. MacConnell as a heartfelt expression of gratitude for his many contributions to education in the Beaverton area.

JAMES J. BLANCHARD, Governor
State of Michigan

TOM ALLEY, State Representative
The One Hundred Fifth District

THE EIGHTY-FOURTH LEGISLATURE
At Lansing
October 5, 1987

The Doctoral Program

The scholarship offered by Dr. Howard McClusky, which enabled me to leave the Beaverton superintendency to work on a doctorate at the University of Michigan, turned out to be a working fellowship. It was paid for out of funds from the WPA, the American Youth Commission and the Michigan State Department of Education.

At the time I agreed to work for Dr. McClusky I knew that he was dedicated to upgrading young people who had potential and the desire to make a contribution to society. But I didn't know that his contacts with influential people, foundations and state and federal government agencies with the same philosophy were nothing less than phenomenal. Dr. McClusky was a human catalyst whose charm attracted potential students who were willing to sacrifice in order to succeed. He and Dr. Arthur B. Moehlman, who were my university advisors, made graduate school interesting, challenging and profitable for me.

Dr. McClusky

I also learned that diplomacy becomes a necessary skill when a graduate student has co-advisors with totally different educational philosophies.

The first assignment on my University of Michigan doctoral fellowship was to go to Lansing, Michigan in January, 1941 and work for three agencies that were engaged in youth studies. Since each agency was helping to finance me, each wanted its pint of blood, and I had three headquarters—the National Youth Administration, the State Department of Education and the State Department of Vocational Education.

Tripartite Alliance

George Fern headed the State Department of Vocational Education at that time and insisted that everyone under his roof conform to his rules and regulations. All desks were to be clean when the employee left for the night. Stray papers on desks were candidates for the wastepaper basket, and Mr. Fern carried out the mission himself. After observing colleagues searching through debris for important documents a few times, I quickly conformed and since that time have seldom left a littered desk to return to the next morning.

It came as a shock when I realized that I had traded the top education position in the Beaverton community for an upgrade that had me reporting to three different agencies that distrusted each other. This situation became a little difficult when each of the agencies insisted that I have a desk in its office, located in different parts of town. Eventually I learned that it was possible to respect and be loyal to people and agencies that have little love for each other. I guess that's the essence of diplomacy.

There were many benefits to the job. One was the opportunity to travel to and become acquainted with Washington, D.C. where the American Youth Commission was headquartered. Another was extensive travelling in many of our Southeastern states.

When on the road, Sundays were set aside for visiting old cemeteries. One epitaph on a wooden tombstone in Macon, Georgia, read: ''Dear Grandpa, he has gone to be an angel.'' But ''angel'' was mispelled ''angle'' and someone had carved the word, ''worm,'' just below it. I also visited a town that exhibited a double barreled cannon on the lawn of its county courhouse, and whose greatest claim to fame was that its fire department had burned to the ground. All of these experiences enriched my limited background.

THE AYC I was assigned to work with the American Youth Commission (AYC) which was undertaking a fact-finding study of the number and location of youth under the age of twenty who were out of school and out of work. Most of the projects on which I worked were concerned with the status of employment and health of youth in the target group. We were doing spot surveys and recording high concentrations of unemployment and furnishing raw data for publications that were widely dispersed—even being reviewed over the radio. I never had hard evidence but feel that those studies provided some accurate data that helped the government gear up the manpower machinery of World War II more rapidly.

Our group consisted of some fifteen people who assisted with collecting and disseminating vital information on the subject of youth and their plight. My colleagues on these projects were people I had only read about up to that time, such as Dr. Reeves of the University of Chicago and Douglas Fairbanks, Jr.

Although I have never been a skilled researcher, I feel that I became better acquainted with fact-finding procedures and effective techniques of evaluation because of that experience with the AYC during the pre-war months.

Just as the AYC study seemed to be progressing to where I could see some of the results of our labor, our group was assembled in Washington, D.C. There we were notified that it was apparent that the United States would soon be involved in a worldwide war and in all likelihood our group would be disbanded. Those who wanted to stay with the project to the end could do so. Those desiring to return to the campus of their choice to pursue their advance degrees would be offered full-time scholarships from the Rockefeller Foundation. The scholarship carried no responsibilities except to finish as soon as possible. I took less than five minutes to make my choice—which was to return to Ann Arbor and complete my doctor's degree at the University of Michigan. To my surprise, I was the only one of our group to accept the offer. Within weeks the bombing of Pearl Harbor occurred and my former colleagues were numbered among those we had been studying as "out of school and out of work."

Decision

Having full time to devote to studying was a new and gratifying experience for me. I had always envied rich people. But to receive a scholarship from a foundation that was created by the wealthy to assist young people gave me renewed faith in successful people who also have a sense of social responsibility.

BACK ON CAMPUS

I not only had time to study, but to talk with other students pursuing the subject of school administration and to really know them as people. We formed a study group that met at homes and at the Rackham Graduate School Center. Also we could spread out our research materials and leave them in our study areas at Rackham until we were finished with them. What luxury that was to me!

Again I witnessed and was a beneficiary of wealth channelled into a project that benefited society in general. Mr. Rackham, who endowed the Graduate School Center, had been an attorney for Henry Ford and a stockholder in the original Ford Motor Company.

Other Students

Fellow students who became lifelong friends included Malcolm Rogers, who later became superintendent of schools at Willow Run, Michigan; Ed Thorne, superintendent at New Haven, Connecticut; Clarence Hinchey, who headed the schools at Schenectady, New York and Mark Bills, who became superintendent at Flint, Michigan, Kansas City, Missouri and Peoria, Illinois.

Graduate work affects people differently. Receiving two advanced degrees from the University of Michigan proved to me that it was possible to compensate for the deficiencies of an early education. Having a bit of tenacity helped also. I came to realize that people I had admired and even feared were little different from me. It also became evident that eligibility for responsible positions was usually determined by having the credentials to apply for the position.

Arthur B. Moehlman

Dr. Arthur B. Moehlman, who was my major advisor, is on my list of influential people who helped shape my career. He was not the most popular professor in the school; as a matter of fact he was disliked by many of his colleagues. Graduate students upon occasion would say that he was mean but he was fair, which meant that he was mean to everyone. This could have been true but to me I had an advisor who was a strong believer in the profession of education. He was an excellent writer and researcher and taught sound study habits.

Dr. Moehlman had many biases and he never compromised his position. It was from him that I learned many important techniques of sound organization and administration. However, I disagreed with him on the subject matter of his course in school and university planning. One of my assignments in his class was to design a secondary school. I argued that educators should be determining the school program while architects should design the facility. He disagreed, and after reviewing my design (which lacked stairs to the balcony of the auditorium) he informed me that I was to receive a "C" for my inability to produce in his course. I responded that we were even—since he had taught a "C" course! Our relationship cooled for a few days.

A Man of Opinion

As an indication of Dr. Moehlman's eccentricity, January was his busy time. He spent it returning Christmas presents, each accompanied by a curt note informing the sender that he couldn't be bought!

As a graduate student I was practically forced by Dr. Moehlman to become a member of the National Council on Schoolhouse Construction, known today as the Council of Educational Facility Planners, International. Membership in the American Association of School Administrators also was a requirement.

I am still an active member of these organizations. In 1979, I was chosen "Planner of the Year" by the Council and in 1981, the American Association of School Administrators designated me as one of the six recipients of "The Distinguished Service Award in Educational Administration". In 1983 I received a 35-year-membership plaque from AASA. Bill Clapp, another Michigander, received a 40-year award. The old gang is thinning out but membership in the association is still large.

Although these awards are symbolic of leadership in my profession, I feel that I have been fortunate to be selected as I am only one of many who are equally deserving of such commendation. Being thus recognized carries with it the obligation to represent my professional colleagues for the remaining years of my active career.

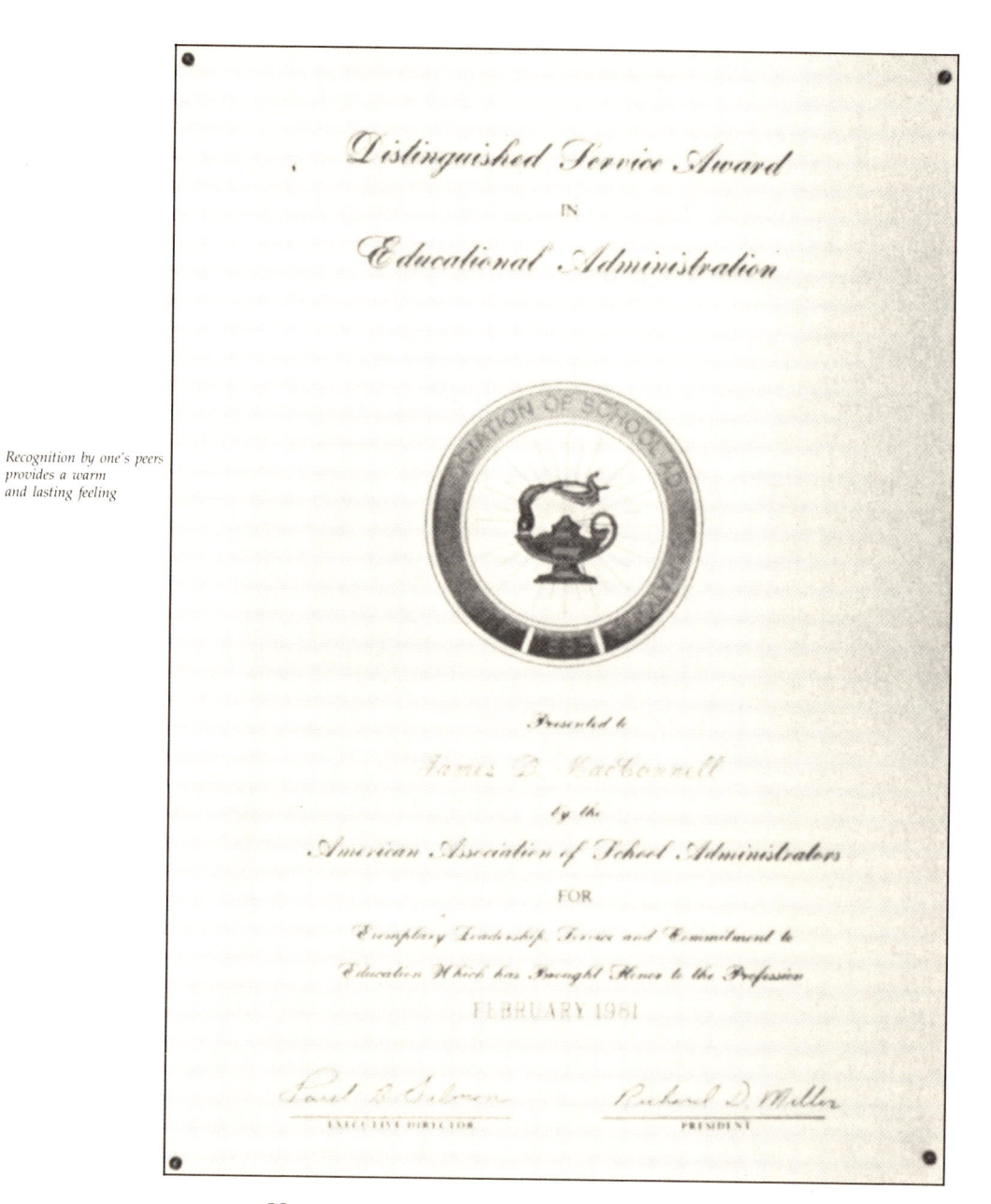

Recognition by one's peers provides a warm and lasting feeling

Distinguished Service Award
IN
Educational Administration

Presented to

James B. MacConnell

by the

American Association of School Administrators

FOR

Exemplary Leadership, Service and Commitment to Education Which has Brought Honor to the Profession

FEBRUARY 1981

EXECUTIVE DIRECTOR   PRESIDENT

A Race with the Draft Board

World War II was well under way when I received notice from my draft board that as I approached graduation, I would be classified "1-A." Choosing a service branch appealed to me rather than depending on the luck of the draw under Selective Service. I discussed the situation with Dr. Moehlman and when he found that I was already thirty-four years old, he advised me to relax since the military was not interested in old men. "This is a young man's war," he said, "and I want you to be superintendent of schools at Saint John's, Michigan." Although I respected Dr. Moehlman's judgement on many things, I felt that this would be an unwise move for me. I would be one of a few men of military age in St. Johns, a city of some 10,000 people about eighteen miles north of Lansing. Also, his definition of a "young man" might not be the same as Uncle Sam's.

The Marine Corps

My next move, which I later found to be not too wise, was to seek enlistment information at the Marine induction center in Detroit. I was greeted there by a two-hundred-fifty pound Marine who, after questioning me about my background, asked me if I hated the Germans and Japanese. I informed him that I didn't hate anybody, and he retorted that I would never make a decent Marine. He advised me on the spot to go across the street to the Navy Recruiting Center. I knew nothing about the Navy but I suddenly knew that it had a higher priority with me than did the Marines.

THE U.S. NAVY

My first contact with the Navy was with the recruiting officer, Commander Lord. After a brief chat, he felt that I would have no problem being inducted as a Lieutenant, Junior Grade. He agreed that I should not be inducted until I had completed my doctor's degree, and set the date some three months hence. I signed all of the papers, and was told

99

I would become a naval officer providing I could pass the physicial exam. Confident that this would be no problem, I went back to Ann Arbor, feeling much more secure, but withheld the information from Dr. Moehlman, my advisor.

Two week after returning home I received orders to report to Detroit the next day for a physical and then go on to Fort Schuyler, New York. My world fell apart. Again I realized that one couldn't always depend upon word of mouth promises, especially when our country was fighting two wars.

Sharing the News

How to share the news with Dr. Moehlman was my next problem as I had essentially violated his considered judgement and advice. Knowing that he would take an occasional drink of bourbon, I hastened to a liquor store and from there to his home. I guess that I should have consumed some of the contents myself, because as I walked by the window of his den I could see him sleeping on his davenport, and I realized that he was not going to receive my news kindly. Mrs. Moehlman invited me in and the hour I waited for him to wake up was perhaps the longest hour of my life.

When Dr. Moehlman finally came out of the den and spotted the liquor, he quickly sized up the situation and barked, "MacConnell what have you done now?" I revealed my misconduct, expressed my regrets, and also informed him that I didn't feel that I was an old man, and that I was determined to go into the military as an officer and not as an enlisted man. His eyes were piercing as he suggested that I report as directed, but ask for the ninety-day deferral before reporting for active duty that had been agreed upon earlier. He kept the bourbon and as I went out the door told me that if the plan didn't work to call him from the recruiting office.

Shark Bait

In Detroit the physical exam went as I anticipated and I was told that after signing some papers I should proceed to Hudson's department store to be fitted for a uniform. At that point I requested of the admitting officer that a ninety-day extension be granted and proceeded to tell him my sad story about needing the time to complete the dissertation for my doctor's degree. The officer was not only unsympathetic, he was downright hostile. First, he explained that we were at war. (Which had we not been, I would not have been there in the first place.) Then, he let me know that I was definitely putting myself ahead of my country, and that if I didn't sign, my name would be forwarded to my draft board and soon thereafter I could be assigned to the Army. He also informed me that should I be fortunate enough to be drafted by the Navy, I would definitely go in as an enlisted man and probably be sent directly to sea. He explained that the non-commissioned Army draftees are used for cannon fodder, but in the Navy they become shark bait.

Feeling like a criminal, I got permission to step out of line long enough to make one telephone call. Dr. Moehlman was nearly as hostile on the phone as the admitting officer, but he suggested that I request a 48-hour period to think things over. The request was grudgingly granted by the officer along with directions to accept by then or that was it.

My dissertation topic, "A Study of Fiscal Capacity in Relation to Public Education in Michigan," was part of a much larger study being conducted under the direction of the State Superintendent of Public Instruction. Dr. Moehlman's approach was to call Governor Kelly and inform him that without an extension of time my part of the study would not be completed.

The next thirty hours were uncomfortable for me, but Dr. Moehlman had laid solid groundwork and the appropriate people performed as requested. On March 29, 1943 my commission was issued and the induction extension granted. I felt somewhat guilty about the whole incident but as a result of the delay in being inducted I was not assigned to a desk job on some base or sent to Armed Guard, which in the Navy was often a one-way ticket.

The dissertation was completed within the extension period and Dr. Moehlman arranged for me to take my final

Moehlman to the Rescue

oral examination on a Sunday after I was in uniform. All the degree hurdles were completed except for the foreign language requirement in Spanish.

I felt as all graduate students do, that my dissertation would be widely read, and be responsible for changing the pattern of financing Michigan schools. Many years later I returned to Ann Arbor and visited the University library to review my magnus opus. Imagine my chagrin to discover that I was the first person to withdraw the document. Since then whenever students at Stanford expressed a desire to write a dissertation that would make a significant contribution, I would commend them with tongue in cheek.

THE DEGREE AT LAST

In the winter of 1943-44 while on an educational mission in New York, my commanding officer requested my presence in his office. I assumed that another upardonable naval crime had been committed, so responded with tribulation. I was surprised to be notified that my commander had received word from Dr. Moehlman that a Spanish language examination was all that was between me and a doctoral degree. I was even more surprised and pleased that he had arranged for me to have a Spanish tutor. Within three weeks I successfully completed the final requirements for the degree.

Few graduate advisors would have gone to so much trouble for a student. Because of Dr. Moehlman's efforts, I was equipped to be considered for any educational position that required a doctor's degree. I am grateful to him. I have always felt that his life would have been longer had he tempered his vendetta against football players, the U.S. Office of Education, and parochial schools.

Into The Navy

On June 28, 1943, with my three-month-old Lieutenant, J.G. commission in the U.S. Naval Reserve, I was ordered to report for indoctrination to the Naval Training School at Fort Schuyler in the Bronx, New York. Fort Schuyler proved to be interesting but confining. I envied the officer and enlisted men teachers who were free to leave the base at 5:00 PM each day for we were permitted only two overnight leaves during the six weeks of indoctrination.

Seeing the sights in New York City was indeed an experience. The lights on Forty-Second Street and Broadway were an eye-opener to me. Long Rapids, which had no street light at all, soon wasn't even a reference point. But I did feel somewhat lost in not being able to speak with people as I met them on the street.

Captain Bartky

After graduation from the training school I was sent to a station in Maryland until a more permanent assignment could be made. I was part of a pool of freshly caught naval reserve officers available for review by senior officers looking for manpower. Soon I was interviewed by a Captain John Bartky of the Bureau of Naval Personnel in the Navy Annex, Washington, D.C. A former school administrator from Chicago, he selected me as a trainer for officers and enlisted men. Being assigned to work in a field in which I felt competent was a lucky day for me. Not only that, my comanding officer was a proven survivor of the educational and political turmoil of a large city system.

I didn't know then, of course, that lady luck would strike five years later when Captain Bartky became Dean Bartky of the Stanford University School of Education, and selected me as Associate Dean.

Lieutenant Timpany

One day as I was standing in line at the Maryland station awaiting assignment, I struck up a conversation with a Navy lieutenant named Russel Timpany who informed me that he had been a school administrator in South San Francisco before the war. On joining up he had rented out his house, parked his wife and baby daughter with relatives, and was ready to be assigned anywhere in the world. As luck would have it, he was sent to San Francisco as a teacher training officer—which was the last place he wanted to go, since he had disposed of his house for the duration. Later Russ Timpany and I became close friends. When I returned from battle zones in the South Pacific, he and his wife, Helen, would provide refuge. Later he became Superintendent of the Santa Clara County, California School System and we remained friends until his death.

SAMPSON NTS

I was assigned to the Sampson, New York, Naval Training Station to be in charge of teacher training. The Sampson experience was demanding, highly educational and extremely frustrating. Thousands of Naval enlisted men were attending a variety of schools at the base located in the Finger Lakes area of New York State. The base was bordered by Lake Seneca, one of the larger lakes of the group, and the weather was similar to that of Northern Michigan—only more so.

Word got around that the water in Lake Seneca didn't freeze. The sailors soon found out that it was because of the extreme depth of the lake and didn't hold true when they put the water in their automobile radiators.

Commodore Batt

Our commanding officer, Commodore Batt, was somewhat disgruntled because he hadn't made Admiral and had little patience with teacher training programs. He was the kind of fellow who demanded salutes of his automobile as he moved about the base. Neglecting to perform this seemingly childish task, especially when it was twenty degrees below zero, cost me a few much needed leaves.

On one occasion when the Commodore visited a class of mine in instructor training for naval officers he told the entire class that the Naval Academy had never had instructor training, and that he felt that it was a total waste of time.

Lieutenant Commander Albertson, to whom I reported, made my stay at Sampson more bearable. Although I was only a Lieutenant Junior Grade, our thinking seemed to follow similar patterns. We would often meet at the officers' club and console ourselves by agreeing that even if the Commodore were impossible and the weather miserable, we could have been assigned to combat on either ocean—a fate that probably would have been worse.

Lt. Commander Albertson

After being assured that the remainder of my naval career would be spent stationed at Sampson, there was not much to look forward to, except possibly a promotion to full Lieutenant. In the Spring of 1944, however, I was ordered to the Bureau of Naval Personnel in Washington for a meeting. After the session, while bidding farewell to some of my colleagues, I passed by Captain Bartky's office. He was talking to a naval commander whom I did not know, and pointing to me said, "He will do it!" I was notified shortly afterwards that I had just been appointed Director of Shipboard Training for destroyers, cruisers, battleships and flat tops, and also that my promotion was being processed.

NEW ASSIGNMENT

Moving to Washington, D.C., seeking housing, and awaiting orders for the new assignment in the South Pacific taxed my patience as well as my confidence in whether or not the Navy really knew what it was doing. While waiting for the other shoe to drop, I was temporarily assigned to review and evaluate the Illiterate Instruction Program at Camp Perry, Virginia. Although located within a stone's throw of historic Williamsburg, Camp Perry was much different in its make-up and purpose. The Navy had been forced to accept a share of non-reader draftees who prior to that time had been absorbed by the Army. In my temporary assignment as "chief of ignorance and director of miscommunication," I supervised the publishing of written and cartoon documents that would be suitable for the recruits who had not been as

Lieutenant MacConnell, USNR

fortunate as those of us who were assigned to improve their lot in life.

My enthusiasm waned near the end of the first month of the assignment after I was summoned to the commanding officer's headquarters and asked to make a progress report. The commandant was a product of Williamsburg before the restoration, and he was rumored to have owned part of the land that was used for the Camp Perry Center. My interview was short. His first question was, "Lieutenant, just what is wrong with these sailors?" My answer was, "Captain, over half of them appear to be unteachable. Their IQ's, most of them anyway, are less than fifty." When asked what an IQ should be, I answered that ideally we would like to see IQ's of around 100, but that they could be a few points lower and the students would still be teachable. His answer was, "Hell, give 'em time. This class has only been here three months!"

Luckily, a few days after that shocking experience, I was ordered back to Washington, D.C. to report to my new assignment in the South Pacific as Director of Shipboard Training.

THE SOUTH PACIFIC

For someone who had become acquainted with the location of the Hawaiian Islands only because of the bombing of Pearl Harbor, the flight to the Island of Guam with orders to report to the cruiser, USS Pasadena was both thrilling and frightening. Encountering gun fire over the island of Rota, just east of Guam, and enduring a long delay in being met by ground transportation after we landed, deepened my suspicion that although this was going to be a new experience it was one that I could well do without. I later learned that Guam Navy personnel had been notified that our plane had been shot down.

I quickly realized that this supposedly peaceful island was a center of military activity and that I was right in the middle of it. That first night I was assigned to a Quonset hut for sleeping quarters, but found that the soft, warm breezes mixed with the peculiar stench of coral made me nauseous. I also learned the next morning that security was not one of the strong points. Some Japanese had infiltrated the ring of Marines who were supposed to be protecting us and had killed two aviators who had been on the plane from Hawaii with me.

Awaiting the arrival of the Pasadena, I was temporarily assigned to the Gazelle, a stationary oil tanker, after being denied permission to come aboard the Missanawa, another tanker. Since several friends I had made prior to leaving the states were on the Missanawa, I was very disappointed. The reason given was that the Missanawa was overcomplement and that I was needed on the Gazelle.

At sunrise the next morning, I was on the deck of the Gazelle looking toward the ship some two hundred yards away that I had wanted to board the evening before. Then at that very moment a two-man Japanese suicide submarine struck the Missanawa and I had the horrible experience of watching some hundreds of naval personnel blown into the air and burned in oil as their ship exploded.

The Missanawa Disaster

I saw a CIC officer friend of mine, who had been with me on the plane to Guam, lying on the dock with some medics working over him. He had been desperately ill on the way out and I had spent much of my time comforting him as best I could. Now, reporting to his first duty, after two years of special training, he had been killed on the very day he boarded his ship. This was but one of many tragic wastes of war. Two days later I was notified that the USS Pasadena had docked at Guam and that I was to be transferred aboard her.

Life on the cruiser, Pasadena, was more enjoyable than on Guam. I discovered that cruisers and battleships are the choice duty assignments if one has to be at sea. However, seasickness plagued me every day I was aboard. Nothing the ship doctors could do seemed to diagnose the cause, let alone remedy it. After my sea duty was over I went to an ear specialist and was told that my trouble was caused by insufficient ear wax.

I will never know if my training efforts bore fruit, but I did learn that school, in any form, is unpopular with a large

USS Pasadena

percentage of people. I was often blamed for the inadequate equipment that had been provided by the Navy as well as the vulnerable position of those who were trying to learn to operate highly sophisticated equipment under the most inappropriate conditions imaginable.

Recalled

Finally I was recalled to Washington, D.C. The experiences in the South Pacific had taken their toll. Death had always been difficult for me to accept, but witnessing it all around me, and often, was unnerving. I felt fortunate in not being injured in any way personally but was greatly saddened by the thought of those who would not be returning, as well as for their families and friends who would never see those men and boys again.

When I left the ship to return to the states, I was escorted to the captain's gig by a delegation of friends. They told me not to think for one moment that the ship had been bombed if I should turn around to say good-bye to my floating home, and notice a cloud of smoke. It would only be the burning of my celebrated lesson plans.

On the way to Washington, I called Lieutenant Timpany from Hawaii and he met me at the San Francisco Airport. Gratefully, I had a few days to recoup as I sat on the Timpanys' deck counting my blessings and trying to imagine what would eventually happen to the world of nations involved in that senseless conflict.

My whereabouts was always determined by Captain Bartky who operated all teacher training activities on land as well as at sea for the Bureau of Naval Personnel. I was ordered as a trouble shooter wherever training activities were being conducted, which included practically every state in the union. When I was assigned to head up shipboard training, both oceans became my floating training centers, but my total time aboard ship was less than the time I spent on land.

The land based training was reasonably effective, but I always thought that training activities conducted afloat left much to be desired. Sometimes I felt like the cross-eyed discus thrower who never threw the discus very far but always had the attention of the audience.

My stay in Washington was short-lived. Very soon I was assigned to the Carribean to evaluate the results of the training I had observed in the South Pacific and to try to devise improved teaching techniques applicable elsewhere.

> As I was having breakfast one morning in San Juan, Puerto Rico, I was joined by a naval officer whose entire face was covered with bandages. I asked what had happened to him. He told me that he had been on the Missanawa in the South Pacific when it was torpedoed. When I told him that I was just off the bow of that ship when it blew up I saw his eyes peer through the bandages and fill with tears as he asked, "What in Hell really happened?"

THE CARRIBEAN

Life in the Caribbean was relaxing since the war in Europe was winding down and we were doing better in the Pacific. Although I consumed little alcohol, the "in" thing to do was to buy liquor in the Caribbean, where it was cheap, and take it to one's friends in Washington, D.C. One time I landed in Florida with what, up to that time, had been the allowable quota of liquor to bring into the country. I was immediately informed by the non-com on duty that the Naval regulations had changed, and that he would have to report me for this violation. He asked for my travel orders and copied down a series of numbers from them that pertained to ordering additional forms. He apologized for having to report me and said that he sincerely hoped that the incident would not damage my career. I told him that I hoped it wouldn't either, knowing full well that the numbers he had copied down had no bearing on my ever being identified as an offender.

> I was beginning to roll with the punches as a naval officer and to accept that way of life as fairly routine. I enjoyed getting together with my colleagues who had been assigned to Washington. The reunions always enriched my knowledge of what was going on elsewhere.

Although things were looking up as far as the war was concerned, they were not that good for me personally. The much quoted statement that "War is Hell" should be expanded to "War is Hell on marriages." My marriage was falling apart. Looking back, I realize that even though I had always tried to be a good provider, I was probably never a good husband. Christine was a high-strung person under stable conditions, and the additional strain of war fostered uncertainties with which neither of us could cope. Eventually we went our separate ways.

Lieutenant Commander Blough

At one time Lieutenant Commander Glenn Blough, a Central Michigan graduate, was assigned to a training station in Boston as was I. A writer and a comedian, Glenn could always see the bright side of life. One Sunday we visited the Boston zoo. As we observed a mother monkey holding a mirror for her young to look at, Glenn pulled out an envelope and wrote on the back of it "A Monkey with a Notion." This phrase eventually became the title of a children's book, which was illustrated by some sailors who had formerly been employees of Walt Disney. Glenn's first royalty check on that book was sufficient for him to purchase a red Oldsmobile convertible.

While at Newport, Rhode Island, Glenn once observed the commandant, Commodore McGruder, addressing the submarine trainees with such statements as "There will be no shoes worn on this base unless they are half-soled. There will be no white flat hats worn before April first." and so on. Before long, Glenn came out with another children's book in which Commodore McGruder appeared as the mayor of a small town named "Be-No." That book also proved to be a winner.

Glenn Blough and JDM Moonlighting(?)

Unlike most skippers, Commodore McGruder did not want to be called "the old man" as was common terminology for the officer in charge whether on land or at sea. The story goes that two sailors who were chipping paint of the deck of a ship docked at Newport harbor saw the Commodore approaching them. One said, "Here comes that old son of a bitch." McGruder reportedly overheard the remark and shouted at the pair, "Which one of you called me old?"

Prior to becoming a naval officer, Glenn had written a grade school geography text as well as a science series. He credited his geography book's success to its size. It was, in fact, physically the largest of any geography book in the United States and provided better protection for students to hide behind!

As a lieutenant, my educational decisions could always be questioned by a lieutenant commander or a higher officer who was not a specialist in my field. Although this bothered me at times, I could see that a successful military organization had to be regulated differently from a civilian group. Key decisions require strict compliance when people's lives are at stake. I also realized that many of the higher ranking officers as Naval Academy graduates were specialists and that the Navy was their lives. By the same token, I knew that if I ever held a key position in a college I, too, would be acknowledged as a specialist in my field. It turned out later, when I supervised the Navy personnel administration and training program at Stanford, that some of those same Marine and Naval officers were enrollees in the program.

I was relieved of active duty on December 16, 1945. The Navy will always be close to my heart. Today, as I see naval vessels pass under the Golden Gate Bridge, I feel proud to have been a part of that service. If nostalgia starts to work overtime, however, I quickly recall the days and nights that I was not only frightened but also seasick. Then I am thankful to be a land lubber.

VANTAGE POINT

It is amazing to realize that as late as 1945 there were no jets, no color TV and no digital computers, yet today millions of us take those things for granted. A passenger jet on an overseas flight today burns more fuel in the first 3 minutes than Lindbergh's plane did on his 22 hour New York to Paris flight. The country's biggest airline boasted in 1940 that it would fly 100,000 passengers that year. The same airline is currently carrying that many passengers every day.

December 19, 1945

To: Lieutenant James D. MacConnell, (S), USNR, 272269

Subj: Commendation.

1. You are hereby commended for outstanding service as the Officer-in-Charge of the Shipboard Training Unit of the Instructor Training Section, Standards and Curriculum Division, Training Activity, Bureau of Naval Personnel, from April 1944 to December 1945 during which time you directed and supervised the program for training junior officers and petty officers in effective teaching techniques to be used aboard ship and in so doing you displayed keen judgment, outstanding initiative, organizational ability, and effective leadership in the performance of duty; and contributed materially to the successful prosecution of the war.

2. A copy of this letter will be made a part of your official record.

(Signed)

William M. Fechteler,
Assistant Chief of Naval Personnel

Post-War Adjustments

Out of the Navy and out of work as a civilian was my status the last two weeks of December 1945. But on January 1, 1946 I joined the Michigan State Department of Education to act as its representative processing requests for War Surplus materials that could be used by universities, colleges and public schools.

That job was to be an excellent stopgap position, as it provided the opportunity to keep in contact with both the Navy and the Michigan State Department of Education and to explore the educational administration opportunities that were becoming available in Michigan and other mid-west states. It was not my idea of a lifetime job, but for the time it served my purposes well.

WAR SURPLUS

The war surplus commodity racket was just that. Every educational organization in the state of Michigan seemed to be writing, telephoning or sending someone in person to inquire about or to examine materials that were available for sale at greatly reduced prices. The materials, some used, many new in original packing, were left-overs which were no longer needed by the military.

The commodities that were warehoused caused much less trouble than those that were listed in catalogs with inadequate descriptions. The great fear on the part of most school representatives was that they would miss out on a bargain that some other district would get. True need became secondary as rumors made their rounds about the steal another school district, hundreds of miles away, had made. There was an added risk in ordering sight unseen because all costs of delivery were to be paid by the recipient.

Grab, Grab

One superintendent from a small Michigan community felt the need for a heating and air conditioning unit for his office that was listed in the surplus catalog. When the unit arrived he received a call from the local station agent saying that his air conditioning unit was on the rail siding and to come down with a school check to pay the transportation charges. The superintendent's shock was justified when he was presented with a freight charge of several thousand dollars for a war plant's air handling unit that had filled a freight car! Our estimate was that this equipment had sufficient capacity to air condition every building in the town. A sadder fact was that the town was in the upper peninsula and could not possibly have needed air conditioning for more than two or three days a year.

I was often shocked while working as a coordinator for the state and federal governments. It took two months of paperwork to arrange delivery of a carload of surplus toilet paper, costing less than one hundred dollars, to the Detroit School District; while in one afternoon we completed the paperwork to sell the entire Willow Run Bomber Plant, including land and runways, to the University of Michigan for one dollar.

Making arrangements to dispose of a couple of horse saddles, left over from some previous war, to a private riding academy consumed reams of paper and resulted in a less than satisfied new owner. Apparently the saddles had deteriorated with age more than the catalog description had intimated.

Heading the military surplus property program gave me an opportunity to reacquaint myself with many of my former colleagues in the state, and also to meet many new educators.

JOB HUNTING

During my spare time on the job, I made contact with both Central Michigan and the University of Michigan employment agencies to find a lucky school district that wanted the services of a school administrator who was in possession of a recent doctor's degree. Dr. Moehlman bypassed the University Placement Bureau, in which he took great delight, and notified four other former graduate student colleagues and me of a vacancy as superintendent at Freeport, Illinois, a city of some twenty-five thousand residents.

My immediate goal was to get that position. Freeport was twice the size of Alpena when I was in high school, and to be superintendent of schools in a city that big seemed like a fantasy. The job was even more attractive when I became aware of the $10,000.00, three-year contract that was being offered. As the School Board's number one choice, Mark Bills, superintendent in Flint, Michigan had been offered the job first. But eventually, the Board in Flint sweetened his salary there, and he decided to stay. His exit from consideration in Freeport made me the number one candidate for the job.

My enthusiasm flagged only a little when the local newspaper headlined my arrival for the interview with the Board as "Inexperienced Former Navy Lieutenant Arrives in Town to Sign $30,000 Contract."

A Minor Item

For all practical purposes I had been hired, but prior to being awarded the contract, the Board of Education requested an interview because as the president of the Board had told me over the telephone, a few minor items had to be cleared up. This was the last of three job interviews I was to have in my career.

The alleged "minor item," which was revealed at the meeting, was that they already had an existing superintendent. This was a Mr. Shaffer, who seated himself across the table from me, and took the position that he had tenure as superintendent and that the Board could not fire him.

I could use all of the space on these pages to describe what happened in the meeting that night. Three of the younger board members wanted new educational leadership to put the Freeport District on the cutting edge—as were some other schools of similar size around Chicago and bordering Lake Michigan. I have often wondered since whether they would have been willing to spend the funds that would have been required to ensure that status.

By midnight the stalemate still prevailed. I had a number of short conversations with Mr. Shaffer while the battle was raging and found that he was an older, conventional educator, but well-grounded in school administration and in the community itself. So my next move was to stand up, trying to make my five-foot-ten inch body look impressive and say, "I withdraw myself as a candidate for this position." That was probably the hardest decision on short notice I have had to make in my lifetime, but it proved to be the correct one.

Superintendent Shaffer took the case to court and it was finally ruled that he did have tenure. Had I been awarded a contract that night, the Freeport School District would have had to deal with the conflicting philosophies of two superintendents for a number of months at least. I am certain, moreover, that with all the bells and whistles that I would have brought to the District, including my unused doctor's degree, Superintendent Shaffer would have been recognized as the educational head of the community.

I was still without a superintendency. There were times while I was in that gray zone of my professional life when I wondered if I would ever find a leadership role that really fit. But I kept filling out application forms for a variety of jobs that I felt I could do. One potential position was negated when I dictated a response to a prospective employer and directed my secretary to sign and mail it for me.

Another Try

What I had written to the president of a school district, with whom I had communicated by telephone, was: "Since you know much more about your school district than I do, I shall await your direction as to my next move." When the Board president did not answer, I went on with my search. Much later, when I moved from Lansing, I was cleaning out my files and ran across the carbon of the letter that had been written and signed by my secretary. It read: "Since I know so much more about your school district than you do, I shall await your direction as to my next move."

One of our neighbor's children returned home from the first day of school and was asked what he learned. His answer was, "Nothing. You know I can't read or write, and now they won't let me talk!"

Back in the Navy

The old saw that the darkest time comes just before the dawn proved true in my case. Late in 1946 I was notified that I had been successful on a civil service exam for the position of "Senior Educationist for the Bureau of Naval Personnel." This meant moving back to Washington to become the top civilian educator for the Bureau.

Returning to Washington was an easy transition. Back in the Navy Annex where Captain Bartky and many of my naval officer colleagues had headquartered, I could see the Pentagon down the hill as well as the Arlington Cemetery across the street from my office window. Until I became oriented to my new responsibilities, I remember feeling that I wasn't making any more contribution than those residing in the cemetery.

As the top civilian in the Bureau, I had the responsibility for guiding the education and training of officers and enlisted personnel for the Navy and Marines. Now a temporary civil service employee, I was in a key educational position that proved to be challenging some times and frustrating at all times. Reviewing proposed additional courses, curriculum changes, new testing techniques, and a variety of other projects were matters with which I initially felt totally unqualified to deal.

SENIOR EDUCATIONIST

Education and training were moving a little higher on the Navy's priority list, as was health, including dental health. One of the enlisted men at Great Lakes expressed amazement that the Navy dentist was so concerned about the condition of his teeth and was heard to remark, "I came into the Navy to shoot the enemy, not to bite them!"

Being the top civilian educator didn't mean much since it soon became clear that I was not always the top decision maker. As a lieutenant in the Navy, I had noted that opinions of those officers with doctorates were highly valued by senior naval and marine officers on practically all subjects including education. That did not always prove to be true, however,

Top Civilian

117

when the possessor of such a credential was a full-time civilian staff member of the Bureau of Naval Personnel.

Often many hours of my time were spent researching factors to be carefully weighed before making an important educational decision, only to find that the decision had already been made by a high-ranking naval or marine officer. I never felt that it was a lack of confidence in me on their parts, but that my billet was new and that decisions had always been made by them in the past. I found the Navy to be like many other organizations, in that duplication of effort is often a result of size.

The Directors

I reported to a captain who held the title of Director of Education for the Bureau. During my tenure, I had two directors, Captain Rice and Captain Ensey, neither of whom was chosen because of his educational background. To the contrary, that choice appointment was a reward for officers who had served the Navy well at sea, and now had earned time on shore with their families.

Captain Rice was a jewel. We both arrived on the scene about the same time. His first statement after we had introduced ourselves was, "Doctor, I hope to Hell you know what this is all about, because I don't."

IMPROVING INSTRUCTION

My general criticism of the performance of Naval officers and enlisted men in all teaching positions was that they were poorly prepared as teachers and selectors and organizers of instructional materials. So I requested, and was granted permission, to mount a project for the improvement of instruction in the Navy.

Although we had indeed won the war in the Atlantic and the Pacific, I was sure that we could have accomplished the task in less time and with fewer lives lost had the Navy paid more attention to training. In short, I felt that if the Japanese couldn't lick us, they couldn't lick anyone. For some reason, the Navy didn't recognize the crucial importance of providing up-to-date training equipment and effective teacher training.

The result was that many poorly trained people put their lives on the line, as well as those of others.

Although there were adequate aptitude and other tests available, it was commonly known that personnel arriving at training centers were often assigned to schools according to the day they arrived at the center. At Sampson NTC, Monday arrivals were assigned to the Cooks and Bakers School, while arriving on Tuesdays practically guaranteed assignment to the School for Gunners' Mates.

Having been the victim of a score of poor teachers, I felt confident in taking a stand on the need to improve instruction. My observation was that the best teaching usually took place in the lower grades in school, while poor performance was too often commonplace by those presenting subject matter in colleges and universities. Usually, the further up the educational scale one went, the less adequate the instruction became.

The NROTC

It was finally decided that the training programs for Naval officers in the areas of Personnel Administration and Training should be divorced from the Navy environment and that at least three centers should be selected at prominent universities to provide such instruction. Since most training was being done in the Naval Reserve Officer Training Centers (NROTC) in some fifty colleges and universities, the new centers would be located at three of those sites.

Because of my position, I was designated by Captain Rice as the chief negotiator in the selection of those centers. To this day I shudder when I hear the word, negotiate. I shall always be amazed at the red tape that cropped up in making selections. To me it wasn't that big a problem, but to both the Navy and the educational institutions, it was a big deal indeed. Ignoring the six months of meetings, telephoning, writing and traveling, Ohio State, Stanford and Northwestern Universities were finally selected as the centers where the courses would be offered.

More Travel

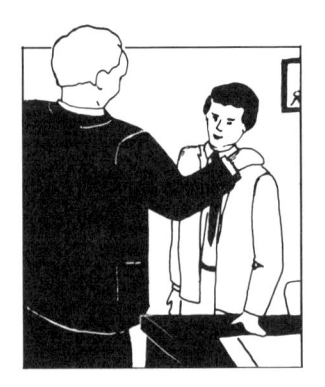

My position required more travel than the excessive amount I had had to do as a Naval officer. Jet travel was nonexistent and each trip across the United States took an entire day. Relaxing train travel, quite popular at the beginning of the war, now had been deleted from my orders. Night flying became common as trouble spots called for tighter schedules.

With bloodshot eyes one morning, after completing an all-night flight, I was scheduled to meet with the six-foot-four-inch tall Vice President of the University of Southern California. I introduced myself as J.D. MacConnell, Senior Educationist for the Bureau of Naval Personnel. He look down on me and smiled as he said, "You aren't old enough to be senior anything." He put his big hand on my shoulder and said, "Young man, let's sit down and discuss this little naval problem; it shouldn't be too difficult for an old vice-president and a young senior educationist to solve." In the following years when I was on the Stanford faculty, even though USC usually gave us strong athletic competition, I always had a soft spot in my heart for the school because of the "old vice-president."

Since a year had been consumed by this time, Captain Rice's shore duty had ended and he returned to sea duty. By now I felt more comfortable in my position and much better qualified to brief my new boss, Captain Ensey, as he assumed the position of Director of Education for the Bureau.

Captain Ensey

I soon was aware that luck was following me around as I became better acquainted with Captain Ensey. From the first, he was complimentary and supportive of my accomplishments. And even though he added more responsibilities to my job, he was the type of person you would work your heart out to satisfy. I soon found myself being consulted on programs that were going to make a real difference in the Navy's future educational policies.

Ultimately, I felt that the Navy's education and training program had a very positive effect on our country. From interesting enlistees in a trade, to launching civilian careers via NROTC and graduate programs, the contribution to society made by the Navy has been significant.

I admired Captain Ensey's philosophy of life as well as his honesty. From him I learned that success was often the result of taking your job, but not yourself, seriously. One example of his philosophy was demonstrated when he was summoned by Admiral Holliway, Chief of the Bureau of Naval Personnel, along with some five other senior officers to explain their version of an incident at sea that resulted in the loss of one of our larger fleet ships. Each officer explained his reason for having little or no responsibility for the tragedy. Captain Ensey's answer, simply was, "Admiral, I have failed. Although I was not totally responsible, had I used better judgment I could possibly have prevented this tragedy from happening." Whether or not this remark was responsible for his being the only one of the six to make Admiral, I'll never know, but I do know that people with his type of character have many things going for them.

> *Social meetings were a welcome relief from the daily crises. One evening during a Christmas party Barney Moran, a Navy civilian, was wildly tossing popcorn throughout the living room where we were all gathered. Mrs. Ensey walked up to him and said, "Barney, I shall never invite you to my home, because of your actions." He looked her in the eye and said, "Mrs. Ensey, from what I have heard about your home, I will not be missing anything." This type of statement would have endangered the position of most civilians responsible to a commanding officer, but the Enseys thought Barney's statement was hilarious.*

In retrospect the scope of my civilian job in the Navy was really quite impressive. As Senior Educationist in the Bureau of Naval Personnel, I was housed in an office adjacent to that of the Director of Education and was responsible for reviewing all aspects of training throughout the Navy and Marine Corps. I made recommendations regarding practically every aspect of training including preparation of audio-visual aids for specific training programs, the selection of encyclopedias and appropriate tests, as well as new courses that the Department of the Navy should consider offering. In addition to programs at temporary training centers like Sampson, New York, where some one hundred thousand enlisted men had been trained, I also was concerned with permanent bases such as Great Lakes Training Center at Chicago, the facility in San Diego and the Naval Officer Training Centers located on college and university campuses. Although the Naval Academy was also under the auspices of the Bureau, I soon learned that one treaded lightly on all aspects of that program.

STANFORD VS. NAVY

By mid-1948 Captain John Bartky had left the Navy to become Dean of the School of Education at Stanford University and had called me regarding my interest in assuming the position of Associate Dean. The decision was difficult. My permanent civil service appointment had just been granted. I was assured of a lifetime position—unless I killed someone or raped an admiral's wife at high noon in front of the officers' club—with a salary of over $10,000.00 per year, while Stanford was offering only $5,600.00. Another complicating factor was that I was becoming more comfortable in the Navy. This bothered me as I knew very well that the Navy belonged to the officers, and that civilians, regardless of their positions, would always be stepchildren. Right or wrong, this was a fact as I viewed it.

Decisions,

Stanford's offer was as an associate professor with only three-year tenure. I would have a maximum of six years to prove that I had the potential to become a full professor. If I were successful, I would have a secure position at Stanford until my sixty-fifth birthday.

During this period of decision making, two of my colleagues-to-be, Dr. Paul R. Hanna and Dr. Robert Bush, visited me and expounded on the advantages of being a university professor. They were confident that the sizeable salary difference could easily be supplemented by educational consulting that was much in demand, especially for professors in the field of school administration.

I knew that risks were unavoidable regardless of the decision I made, so long range job satisfaction and possible professional contributions dominated my thinking as the time of decision drew near.

Decisions, Decisions

A trip to Stanford to talk with Dean Bartky and President Alvin Eurich played a key role in my decision to entrust my future to Stanford. Agreement that I would be permitted to be away from the campus two days per week for consulting work, providing I taught Saturday classes, was a contributing factor that tilted the scales toward Stanford. This would be the first time that I had the opportunity to practice the advice Mr. Gallup gave when I was starting my career: "Your profession should always be your top concern, but you probably will never be financially comfortable in education unless you do some diversifying. Reserve at least twenty percent of your time for yourself."

My parting interview with Captain Ensey's boss, Admiral Black, was difficult. After presenting my reasoning, and seeing it shot full of holes by the admiral, I said goodbye. His final shot was, "MacConnell, there have been times when I have questioned your decisions, and now I am convinced that I had good reason to."

I had made key professional decisions before, but none so critical as this one. No doubt I was as well qualified as anyone in my profession to be Senior Educationist for the Bureau of Naval Personnel. I was the top civilian educator and had literally hundreds of other educators, and many top Naval officers under my jurisdiction. I had but one Naval officer to report to, and nearly total security.

My much shakier alternative was to venture into the professional field of higher education where financial security was nearly non-existent beyond three years when I could be considered for tenure. At that point, providing I measured up in the judgment of my colleagues, I could be on the top rung of the academic ladder and have a lifetime opportunity to make major contributions to my chosen profession. I opted for Stanford and have never regretted the decision.

Midway in my civilian Navy career, on June 17, 1947, I married June Ruff of Miverva, Ohio. I had met June at the

June in June

Naval Training Station at Sampson, New York, during the war where she was a civilian employee at the base.

After I was reassigned June would occasionally write and bring me up to date on the happenings in the lives of many of our Sampson acquaintances. Often she would spice up the letters by including a few stories that I could share with my colleagues during the unproductive hours aboard ship while we were waiting for something to happen.

June thought that I might be a workaholic but took the risk in marrying me. She was convinced of the correctness of the appelation when I cut short our honeymoon in Bermuda to return to Washington, D.C. to put out a small fire.

Although she loved Washington, D.C., when the evaluating process was under way to decide to stay with the Navy or to go to Stanford, she agreed that the move to Stanford would be the one with which she would feel most comfortable.

The reduction in salary was a bothersome factor to both of us. But since she had graduated from a business college in Cleveland I told her that if Stanford were to be our choice, I would buy her a typewriter and a mirror and she could make a choice between typing dissertations or watching herself slowly starve to death. Financially we witnessed some uneasy moments in the early Stanford years, so the dissertion typing became a relied upon income supplement.

June

I always have felt that June dreamed that living in a large house on University Avenue in Palo Alto, and my coming home for lunch each day would be an idyllic life. To this day I think that as she drives down University Avenue she enjoys the years she never spent living there, much as I re-live the imaginary rose garden party for my parents that never took place.

Although we didn't get the University Avenue address we did build a house on a dream four-acre plot in the hills overlooking Stanford lands. There young deer eat June's newly planted shrubs, while their parents check with our gardener to determine if we should be eliminated from their hit list for the following season.

Stanford University Hoover Tower from Quad

Cubberley School of Education Building

125

STANFORD UNIVERSITY

OFFICE OF THE PRESIDENT

STANFORD UNIVERSITY, CALIFORNIA
May 21, 1948

Professor James D. MacConnell
School of Education
Stanford University

Dear Professor MacConnell:

At the meeting of the Board of Trustees of Stanford University held on May 20, 1948, you were appointed as Associate Professor of Education for a five-year period beginning September 1, 1948 at a salary of $5,600 for the year 1948-49.

Under this appointment it is assumed that you will teach during three quarters of each year and devote the fourth quarter to research and writing.

It will be a pleasure to welcome you to Stanford.

Sincerely yours,

Alvin C. Eurich
Acting President

P.S. Delighted you are joining us

The beginning of a wonderful experience.

Down On "The Farm"—25 Years at Stanford

When my appointment in September, 1948 as an associate professor of education had been signed by the president of Stanford University, it seemed like a dream to me—a dream that I only hoped I could afford. It did a lot for my ego. To me it was an entre into the real world of education at its highest level. It seemed that all the steps in my career, the preparation, the experience and the luck, were finally linking together. Although Dr. Alvin Eurich, the president hardly knew me as a lieutenant in the Navy, he was Dean Bartky's superior officer and knew that I was one of Bartky's boys.

"The Farm" as countless generations of graduates have lovingly called Stanford—or more correctly Leland Stanford Junior University—derives from the farm land, the University founder, railroad magnate, California governor and senator, donated as a site for a Harvard of the West named in honor of his young son who had died as a teenager.

Changes at the School of Education

The aftermath of the war was being felt at Stanford as it was in most universities in the United States and the free world. Stanford's faculty was made up of two groups, those who had stayed on campus during the war and those who had served in the military. Although there were some indications by a few stay-at-homes that the military people had been too long out of touch with academia, for the most part we were welcomed into the ranks as colleagues who would share the responsibility of pulling together what was left of a school of education that had distinguished itself under the leadership of its former dean and founder, Elwood P. Cubberly.

Additional Staff

New members were being added to the staff of Stanford University School of Education (SUSE) to fill vacancies and newly created positions that represented the new era in higher education. Personnel, finance, teacher education, placement and other specialized disciplines and service areas offered marvelous opportunities for those of us who joined the faculty at that time.

In addition to my duties as associate dean, I had to choose a field of concentration and offer courses that would help qualify students for master's, specialist's and doctor's degrees in education.

FACILITIES PLANNING

The need for expert educational facilities planning had been an interest of mine since my days with Dr. Moehlman at the University of Michigan. Now I saw a real opportunity to help Stanford School of Education graduates develop skills in the area of functional and modern planning for educational facilities. The idea of creating structures that would actively assist the learners made a lot of sense, but of course, had not at that time been accepted as part of the academic offerings in major universities.

Planning, as a field of study, was not viewed with great enthusiasm at first, but there was an acknowledged need to expand the administration curriculum in the School of Education. Some of the pure academicians on the faculty would have been more comfortable had this semi-vocational area of interest been established at San Jose or Chico State Colleges instead of Stanford. As I was associate dean, however, they apparently chose not to register their protests in the formative stages of building an additional department.

I often felt that I had projected myself into a no win situation and thought of comedian Foster Brooks' lines before a Chicago audience when I was present: "You all know that I have been married twice. My first wife died from eating poison mushrooms. My second wife passed away as the result of a skull fracture because she refused to eat poison mushrooms."

The first faculty meeting I attended at Stanford provided a clear indication that pure academics was the highest item on the priority list of most of the thirty members of the School of Education faculty.

Stanford Vs. Michigan

Stanford presented many interesting contrasts with my alma mater. The University of Michigan offered the traditional doctoral degrees, Ph.D. and Ed.D. At the beginning of the second year of the doctoral program, candidates would choose the Ph.D. if they were oriented to research and were willing to take two foreign languages and additional courses in psychology and statistics. Those candidates often would become college and university professors.

Those candidates more oriented to the practitioner field would take only one foreign language, and would specialize in school management and organization courses. They would write their doctoral dissertations in some area that would better prepare them to be school administrators.

At Michigan, dissertation topics would usually be assigned by the major professors, after a brief discussion with the candidate. I was assigned to determine the fiscal capacity of school districts to support public education. Assigning the topic consumed all of fifteen minutes, and I was told to get on with it. At Stanford, selecting a dissertation topic frequently took from six months to a year and often the candidate and committee were unable to agree on a topic, resulting in many students going through life with the "ABD" degree—All But Dissertation.

ABD Degree

That difference between Michigan and Stanford was high-lighted at the first SUSE staff meeting. One of my collegues, Dr. Larry Thomas, opened the faculty meeting with the topic, "The Difference Between the Ed.D. and the Ph.D. Degrees." The general discussion centered around ways to make certain that the Ed.D. was difficult, and thereby as prestigious, as the Ph.D. As it happened my last faculty meeting, some twenty-five years later, was also chaired by Larry Thomas. Over the years, Larry had become a respected colleague and a recognized student of philosophy. At my last meeting, too, Larry was leading the discussion on "How the Ed.D. should differ from the Ph.D."

I suspected that at first Dean Bartky favored my decision to cast my lot in the planning field because it was different. Later, he began to feel that it might be too different, and that

SCHOOL PLANNING LABORATORY

its rapid expansion could cause dissension among the faculty. He reminded me that a venture of this kind could only survive if it became recognized as a sound educational program throughout the country. I decided that that could only be accomplished by the creation of a "School Planning Laboratory" (SPL) where theory could be tested and put into practice. First I found a couple of rooms in the basement of the Cubberly School of Education building in which to install the laboratory. They were filled with volumes of old research reports, toilet paper, broken chairs, and a variety of other items of questionable use. Next I notified the faculty to remove the fire hazard or I would. Some responded quickly and positively, but others never forgave me for disposing of research reports containing data that might have been welded into an earth-shaking study.

Little did I know then that it took a lot more than physical space, a few ideas, and personal determination to install a new element in an academic program at Stanford. My courses in school planning and social interpretation, along with the routine tasks of Associate Dean, took most of my time. One class was usually scheduled for Saturday mornings. However, in accord with Mr. Gallup's advice, I had two days during the week when I was responsible only to myself. During my first year at Stanford, I used this time to think through an organization that would function academically, and still be practical to school administrators who were basically "thing thinkers."

Faculty Support

The idea of a laboratory that did not run white rats through a maze was difficult for most of the staff to visualize. One of my colleagues suggested that the Lab would have a better chance of success if I would arrange to leave a couple of holes in the wall close to the floor, enabling white rats to wander in occasionally from the psychology lab next door.

In the beginning, the Laboratory was actually more of a display center where school administrators could come and view school furniture, various lighting fixtures, air handling equipment, flooring, and other innovations such as carpet and colored chalk boards for schools.

The Laboratory evolved and by the fall semester of 1950, it was evident that there was a real need for such a facility and that it should be housed in a school of education that had a position of nationwide status. Consequently, I did everything in my power to make it an integral part of the School of Education School Administration program.

As set forth in the Self Study Report of the School of Education faculty in 1961, "The Program in School Administration...was concerned with the preservation and integration of knowledge about educational administration, its increase through research, its dissemination through teaching and publications, and its application through service to the schools of the nation..." Our program embraced all three areas.

Part of School Administration

The School Planning Laboratory provided an opportunity for doctoral candidates in administration to gain clinical experience in a setting quite different from that provided by typical internships. Candidates who thought they might specialize in school or university planning were especially encouraged to make use of the Laboratory.

The possibilities for development were never far from my mind. Once the display center was available, the next move was to promote a total remodeling progam, including air conditioning, that would provide seminar space, office for graduate students and a well-appointed office for the director.

Although I never officially was appointed director of the Laboratory, I had learned from earlier experiences that impressive stationery and an attractive business card would help bridge between being Associate Dean and the Director of the School Planning Laboratory. Thus I eliminated some of the red tape involved in creating a new department.

Research in the School Planning Laboratory was launched in 1951 with these stated purposes: 1) To determine what classroom environment best promotes the desire to learn; 2) To discover how to eliminate forces that impair children's health, hinder their development, and reduce their ability

Objectives

to learn; and 3) To test ideas for improving the functional aspects of school facilities and to disseminate information on those ideas that prove workable. Those basic purpose were always served, even as the functions of the Laboratory gradually expanded.

Early on, the School Planning Laboratory conducted studies for various communities whose population expansion mandated increased school facilities. Those studies continued to be one of the Lab's chief functions. Additionally, a number of industrial studies were made for companies engaged in manufacturing school furniture and other equipment.

Although the activities of the Planning Laboratory did not always please Dean Bartky, for the most part I had his backing.

EXIT THE ASSOCIATE DEAN

In 1953, one of my colleagues with high academic standards and mixed feelings about my area of concentration, Professor I. James Quillen, replaced Dean Bartky and held the deanship until his resignation for health reasons in 1966.

Dean Quillen and I had a few disagreements regarding the quality of the research projects and doctoral dissertations being written under my advisorship. However, he was fair and I felt that he was generally sympathetic toward my efforts. This may have been influenced by the fact that finances were hard to come by in the School of Education and the field of planning opened doors for fellowships for graduate students.

In December, 1953, I was summoned to Dean Quillen's office and notified that he desired to experience all of the problems a dean should deal with, and was therefore eliminating the position of Associate Dean which I had filled for five years. He said that he would go with me to the President and explore the possibilities of my gaining employment of a similar nature elsewhere.

I explained to him that I was an associate professor and chose to remain at Stanford. He countered that he would have to cut my salary by $2,000 per year. I still would not agree to go elsewhere and from then on became a full-time associate professor. Soon thereafter I moved my office into the Planning Laboratory and depended upon consulting work to replace the $2,000 that I gave up with the associate deanship.

In retrospect the move was a propitious one as it gave me additional time to devote to facilities planning when the need for such was burgeoning. And two years later I was appointed a full professor.

GROWTH OF THE "LAB"

The physical growth of the basement Laboratory was piecemeal. The first four areas and the lobby were completed by 1951, and three additional areas between 1953 and 1955. Originally devoted to displaying school building materials, furniture, and equipment, most of the space after 1951 was used by graduate assistants and staff as an area for work and research. So, the original concept of the Laboratory was expanded and made part of a more comprehensive research and project center being developed on the first floor of the School of Education building.

My philosophy of having the Lab put its best foot forward came into play during the remodeling which included an office for me that equaled the dean's in size and decor. President Sterling visited my office shortly after it was completed and as he left mentioned that if it were centrally located on the campus, he would consider exchanging offices with me.

In spite of the fact that the Stanford School Planning Laboratory was making progress and was being recognized as an integral part of the School of Education, there were a number of problems in the early years. One was that we were a small staff consisting only of a graduate assistant, an underpaid secretary and myself. Another was that we were not considered an organization of long standing either on or off the campus.

Summer Planning Institute

We did have some early wins, however. A key activity that brought attention to the Laboratory and the University was a popular series of summer conferences in planning for education facilities at all levels. The institutes began in 1950, and became well recognized as the best program to attend if you were an architect, a school planner or a school superintendent facing a building project. Every aspect and level of planning was dealt with in one form or another at the institutes. Topics varied from new concepts of maintenance and operation to planning facilities to accommodate newer concepts of curriculum and school organization. The institutes were usually held in late July, and the attendance varied with the nature and popularity of the subject matter being presented. Most institutes drew more than one hundred educators and on two different summers there were more than two hundred conference participants.

It was with surprised delight at one institute that I rescued a custodian who had gotten in the wrong line and found himself a full-time graduate student in the school of Education. This proved to me that even great universities are not infallible, a belief that was strengthened a couple of years later when Ted Dixon, one of my doctoral students received his diploma in the mail prior to completing his dissertation.

Although many people talk about how much better schools were fifty years ago, I don't feel that way. Teachers today are better trained and much more knowledgeable than they were during that era. I remember teaching biology in the thirties. At that time biology was a study of death. It seemed that we caught and pickled everything that showed any sign of life. I'm sure that some students thought that frogs, snakes and fish were born in alcohol. Today, teaching biology is teaching life.

Caring for and learning about living things in elementary and secondary school science laboratories is a marvelous improvement over what used to be.

Enter the Ford Foundation

A significant development in the Lab resulted from luck as well as my being somewhat alert to what was happening in my chosen field of concentration. An article appeared in the San Francisco Chronicle early in 1959 about the Ford Foundation's decision to establish the Educational Facilities Laboratories headquartered in New York City. As stated in the Chronicle, the goals of this venture were practically identical with those that we had adopted at Stanford. I also knew that Alvin Eurich, who had left the presidency of Stanford, was Chairman of the Board of the Ford Foundation. Within a couple of days I was on a plane to New York to ask Dr. Eurich if Stanford's School Planning Laboratory could be a part of the program of the Ford Foundation's Educational Facilities Laboratories.

Dr. Eurich suggested I visit Dr. Harold Gores, formerly business manager and then Superintendent of Schools at Newton, Massachusetts, who had just been selected as president of the Educational Facilities Laboratories. Since Harold Gores proved to be a man with background and interests similar to mine, my conferences with him were a delight. Although he had to await a final decision by the Board, he reacted very favorably to designating our Laboratory as the Western Regional Center of the newly created Educational Facilities Laboratories.

Not knowing quite what to expect, I had taken two proposals to Newton: a full scale version asking for three hundred thousand dollars, and a limited version priced at fifty-seven thousand dollars. Funding was not mentioned in the early stages of our conversations, but before leaving I presented my less ambitious proposal. I was convinced that a new giveaway program, focused on a profession where money was usually a scarce commodity, wasn't about to take

CONTACTS

a flyer with the greater amount. This was especially true as the new president knew little about me and nothing but what I had told him about the Stanford Laboratory.

EFL GRANTS

Our visit with Dr. Gores paid off and a start-up grant was received. After the initial grant, funds for varying amounts were requested from the Educational Facilities Laboratories and granted to the Laboratory. The funds were directly responsible for putting the Laboratory, and on many occasions the entire School of Education, in a leadership role in the field of educational space planning. The goal was always to enable facilities to better accommodate the teaching process in educational institutions from kindergartens through universities.

Well-handled money attracts additional funds. Between the time the first grant was received and my retirement in 1973, several millions of dollars were channeled through Stanford and expended for a wide variety of planning activities.

Half of my salary was picked up by the grants as well as the full salary of a secretary for the Laboratory. Adequate travel funds were provided, as were increased stipends to help graduate students better concentrate on their academic pursuits. The Dean was soon distributing my School of Education travel allocation to other staff members because my EFL travel funds exceeded those of the entire School of Education. The director's office, created from a junk room, became the chosen spot for qualifying interviews for graduate students. Our formerly underpaid secretary, Peg Maule, became one of the better-paid secretaries in the University. Her presence also benefited our graduate students who began to feel that they had gained some prestige in the field of school administration by being affiliated with the Laboratory. Peg's eighteen years as my secretary and colleague were filled with significant contributions to the School of Education.

Research Reports

Before the Ford Foundation's Educational Facilities Laboratories began its relationship with us, it had been practically impossible for the Stanford School Planning Laboratory to pay for the publication of the results of its research and field studies. It was the boost from the Educational Facilities

Laboratories that resulted in the eventual world-wide impact of our work. In May, 1959, the first Stanford SPL (School Planning Laboratory) Report was published. From then on, the Reports were usually published quarterly, and distributed free of charge to some five thousand school people throughout the world.

SPL REPORTS

PLANNING NEW SCHOOLS
JUNIOR COLLEGE–HIGH SCHOOL–ELEMENTARY

THIS ISSUE of *SPL Reports* discusses schools that have opened during the past year. The schools represent elementary, high school, and junior college education. Each school was selected due to its innovative use of interior space and architectural design.

The School Planning Lab reports were of importance in alerting school districts to the increased impact that the baby boom was having on primary schools throughout the country, and what would be happening to enrollments not only in elementary and secondary schools, but also in community colleges and universities.

Although the doubting Thomases dominated in most situations, many educators began calling on the Laboratory for demographic assistance, information on better building utilization, construction cost comparisons, and requesting that we issue Lab Reports advising on those problems. School Planning Lab Reports covering such topics as "Flexible Schools Through Flexible Scheduling," "High School to House Team Teaching in Utah," and "The Walls Come Tumbling Down," drew requests for hundreds of reprints.

For the first time in history a major foundation provided adequate funds to make a difference in facilities planning,

Facing the Baby Boom

an area ripe for help. With the support of Ford Foundation money, the Educational Facilities Laboratories became recognized as a publisher and distibutor of readable, well-illustrated publications in planning for, and in some instances actual planning of, educational facilities. Information was disseminated widely throughout the United States, Canada and many other countries. As Harold Gores used to say, ''If it is concerned with education and you can kick it, Educational Facilities Laboratories is interested in it.'' Many worthwhile educational projects have been financed by numerous foundations, but there is no doubt that the Ford Foundation's Educational Facilities Laboratories led in an area that had been overlooked by nearly everyone else.

SPL Services

As the Stanford School Planning Laboratory grew, so did its list of services available to schools and industries. They soon included consultation on new building site selection, population projections, master planning, the development of educational specifications, school products research, general educational consulting and coordination of educational conferences.

The Planning Functions

The Stanford School Planning Laboratory became known as a center where educators and lay people could come to discuss their local educational facility problems. The very idea of planning for schools was a new thought for many. Teachers who inquired about my classes would typically hesitate before enrolling. They would usually tell me that they were not architects, and my response was that that was in their favor since we would be primarily concerned with the *functions* that they planned to conduct in and around the school. In turn, the resultant educational specifications would be utilized by the architects who were ultimately responsible for designing schools. My experiences with Dr. Moehlman at Michigan had emphasized the necessity of knowing the school program before becoming involved in design.

MASTER PLANNING AS A NEW CONCEPT

In the early nineteen-fifties the concept of looking into the future for guidelines for the long term educational needs became paramount for small school districts that suddenly became large. As "war babies" began to appear on the school rolls, demographic studies were needed to determine the number of students that would eventually result from the couples moving into new housing developments.

It soon became evident that a systematic approach was necessary if long-range educational housing needs were to be met. Policy decisions had to be made in advance by boards of education and college and university trustees as to grade organizations, sizes of classes, anticipated total buildings needed, their location and size as well as the funding required if economically sound procedures were to be practiced. Thus the master plan concept was born.

> Land for school sites in California escalated in price from hundreds of dollars per acre in the early fifties to thousands and even hundreds of thousands of dollars per acre by the mid-seventies. Over a period of years Eastside School District in Santa Clara County saved millions of taxpayer dollars by buying some ten high school sites recommended in a master plan drawn up in the fifties.

Site Selection Problems

A book could be written on the intricate dynamics involved in site selection, often having little to do with choosing the most suitable site. An excellent example is the problem of negotiating with fifty farmers who owned that many small parcels of land, which taken as a group would be well suited as a site for a proposed new American School in Tokyo. All the land owners except one would agree on the number of Yen they would sell for, and when the holdout's request for more Yen would be granted, all the others would raise their prices and another negotiating session would result.

Another example is that of a community where a poor site for a school with a lighted football field was selected over a superior site. In the superior location the lights from the football field would reflect into the mayor's bedroom window!

One reads about bribes and tends to associate them with some types of big business or with the Mafia. I had the experience of being offered a Cadillac convertible by a land developer who was attempting to persuade me that there were other more suitable parcels for a school site than the one our study indicated was the most appropriate.

Site Criteria

It is difficult to relate to the public the incredible range of factors that were considered when school site selections were made by a board of education. Essential data were assembled on the site under study such as: drainage, ease of site preparation, availability of gas, electricity, water and sewer, zoning, and of course the purchase price. Other factors considered included accessibility of the site, availability and problems of acquisition, environmental impact, hazards, present or planned land use, nearness to present or future population centers, and the influence of overall topography.

Site Selection Profile

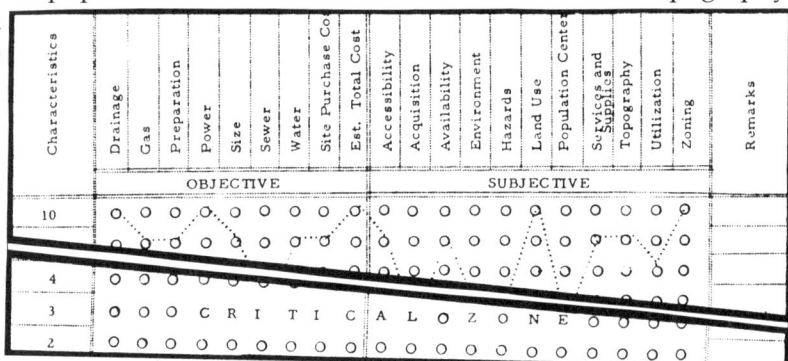

Characteristics	Drainage	Gas	Preparation	Power	Size	Sewer	Water	Site Purchase Co.	Est. Total Cost	Accessibility	Acquisition	Availability	Environment	Hazards	Land Use	Population Center	Services and Supplies	Topography	Utilization	Zoning	Remarks
	OBJECTIVE									SUBJECTIVE										
10	o	o	o	o	o	o	o	o	o	o	o	o	o	o	o	o	o	o	o	o	o
	o	o	o	o	o	o	o	o	o	o	o	o	o	o	o	o	o	o	o	o	o
4	o	o	o	o	o	o	o	o	o	o	o	o	o	o	o	o	o	o	o	o	o
3	o	o	o	C	R	I	T	I	C	A	L	o	Z	O	N	E	o	o	o	o	o
2	o	o	o	o	o	o	o	o	o	o	o	o	o	o	o	o	o	o	o	o	o

These factors, as well as others, were plotted in graphic form to lend a degree of objectivity to data presented to a school board to aid it in its decision. Statistical values were given to the various factors and a site index calculated. Frequently topographic maps were employed to locate proposed or alternative sites to help visualize the positive and negative factors of different locations.

One of the most effective tools was a graph that set forth the economy of early site selection in a growing school district. Factors shown included estimated land cost at the present and at a future date, the negative impact of loss of tax revenue by acquiring privately held property, and the interest cost of early acquisition. Crossover points were plotted which showed the breakeven point of the number of years in advance of use that it would be economical to acquire a site.

Planning for the necessary acreage and proper location of educational facilities was step number one for boards, administrators and teachers, and often lay participants.

The next step was for consultants, educators, and architects to plan *for* schools and then plan the buildings. Schools and colleges had taken over many educational responsibilities that had previously been assumed by parents and other community service organizations. It was therefore important that curriculum and facilities be planned for such activities. Electronics, special education, computer training, pre-school classes and a variety of community adult courses were being conducted in spaces that were not built to accommodate such activities. Consequently, graduate students were being alerted to the present and anticipated curriculum changes that would affect the size and function of such educational facilities.

Some school boards saw "innovative curriculum" reforms such as team teaching and flexible scheduling only as a means of cutting costs. For the most part, however, the idea of grouping students and emphasizing individual instruction was being looked upon as a better educational mouse trap.

Soon school boards, boards of trustees, citizen groups and professional educators were being scheduled into the School Planning Laboratory on a regular basis. Graduate students were becoming consultants to a variety of interest groups and the Stanford Lab became a vital discussion topic as educators and architects gathered throughout the country.

I would like to think that we were forward looking in choosing the field of facility planning as a major interest. This was not the case. We were lucky to be in the right place at the right time to provide a service just as the need for it expanded explosively.

FUNCTIONAL PLANNING

Designing For Function

An important area of consulting on school facilities is referred to as functional design, or programming, or preparing educational specifications. In the past, lack of careful consideration of the potential uses of the educational facility, both building and site, had been both expensive and frustrating to the users of the completed facility.

Often spaces allocated to accommodate specified functions were unrealistic and improperly sized. Frequently the interrelationships of the different types of spaces within a building had been given little if any thought. These situations were more pronounced in expanding districts where trained planners were not a part of the staff, or when those who were aboard were loaded with additional duties.

Although we had been teaching this aspect of planning in classes at Stanford and in the summer school institutes, there were still many administrators and board members who had not been exposed to the planning approach. Hence the need for the School Planning Laboratory to provide consulting services grew almost exponentially during the time of burgeoning school construction.

EDUCATIONAL SPECIFICATIONS

Involving the potential users of the school facility in its planning was important in order to get their programming input. Moreover, a substantial amount of time was necessary in order to plan well. The old adage that "haste makes waste" was apropos. Another was, "To fail to plan is to plan to fail." Regardless of how small the square footage being built, it definitely was too expensive if it had little or no use afterwards because it did not meet the needs of the instructors and students.

Details of the preparation of educational specifications encompass several college courses; however, the major process includes: 1) Analyzing the function of the school facility, i.e. describing the current or proposed school program; 2) Relating the function of the program to the basic factors of school planning; and 3) Describing, suggesting and illustrating the facilities that would encompass the functions of the facility and the basic factors of school planning.

Such information provides a description of the basic elements needed by the architect designing the new facility, and results in a finished product that assures a functional environment for teaching and learning. A more detailed discussion of educational specifications may be found in MacConnell, James D., *Planning For School Buildings*. Englewood Cliffs, N.J.: Prentice Hall, Inc., 1957.

The Lab was not the fountainhead for all school planning as there were a few other colleges and universities also taking leadership roles. The program at the University of Tennessee, headed by Dr. John Gilliland, is a good example. We enjoyed the cross-fertilization of ideas that came from other institutions that were responding to the growing demands for planning for better schools as the youngsters from the baby boom appeared.

SCSD—A SIGNIFICANT CONCEPT

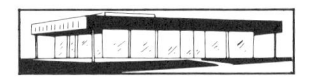

In late 1963, Educational Facilities Laboratories, Inc. launched a project that became one of its major contributions —the School Construction Systems Development (SCSD). Today, the Credit Union building on Stanford's campus is evidence that a building can be constructed not only to accomodate educational activities but to be readily adapted to other uses as well.

Although some great strides had been made, there was still a need for some agency to undertake a project that would focus on the better utilization and arrangement of spaces within the exterior walls of a structure. Such a project would have to be undertaken by an impartial organization that had adequate financing, was experimental to the point that losses could be chalked up to experience, and prestigious enough to have the support of educators, architects, and the manufacturers of building components and school equipment.

That type of project appeared to be ideally suited for the Ford Foundation's Educational Facilities Laboratories.

Led by President Harold Gores and Vice-President Jonathan King, an excellent writer and one who understood art, architecture and education, the project was launched at

Stanford as a joint effort by the Stanford School Planning Laboratory and the Department of Architecture of the University of California at Berkeley. Project Coordinator was John Boice, a graduate student who later used the project as a dissertation for his doctorate. Ezra Ehrenkrantz, an imaginative architect from England, headed the design area.

Integrated Building System

The SCSD project was designed to provide school districts and architects with an integrated system of construction components which could 1) Provide architects design flexibility in meeting changing program needs of schools; 2) Reduce the cost of school construction and maintenance, and 3) Reduce the time needed to build a school.

SCSD enlisted thirteen school districts building twenty-two schools to participate in the project which involved manufacturers willing to conduct research on new materials and equipment with the assurance that a large enough contract would result to enable them to recover costs of their R and D. The SCSD developed a set of performance specifications for the required building components such as structural elements; lighting and ceiling systems; ventilating and cooling systems; and fixed and flexible interior partitions. The ultimate goal was to provide architects with components that were architecturally neutral so that architects could utilize them in any combination with the assurance that the finished product would provide for ultimate flexiblity as uses of the space changed over the years.

The SCSD program resulted in planning *for*, designing, and building some thirty million dollars worth of schools in California using the components as specified in the system's approach to planning and building.

Although the use of components was not new in school building, the SCSD was the first attempt at total systems planning. While some architects felt that their design skills were being encroached upon, most architects, educators and manufacturers cooperated. The process resulted in some new planning techniques for future educational facilities where function of a facility was high on the priority list.

SPL Consulting at Stanford

The Stanford School Planning Laboratory in addition to offering courses, institutes and publications did a substantial amount of consulting and developed a number of master plans. Three of the projects are worthy of mention because of their uniqueness as well as their geographic location and extreme climatic differences. They are the American School in Rio de Janeiro, Brazil, the University of Alaska and the new facilities in American Samoa.

THE AMERICAN SCHOOL IN RIO

The Educational Facilities Laboratories was established by the Ford Foundation to concern itself with educational facility planning in the United States only. It was, however, often requested to represent the Ford Foundation in specific educational planning projects abroad. The American School in Rio de Janeiro, Brazil, was such a project and Stanford School Planning Laboratory was designated to spearhead it.

The project was intriguing for it was my first introduction to Brazil and the environmental differences that had to be considered when planning *for* the new facility.

The first trip brought out the fact that board members acted just like their counterparts in this country—proud of their school and concerned about finances. A site had been selected before we arrived. It was on a 60-degree slope and was bisected by a stream from a waterfall coming down the mountain. The Ford Foundation had suggested that I say something encouraging about the site. I did. I complimented them on the drainage!

My intitial suggestion was that an architect from the United States be employed who was familiar with functional educational planning. The second recommendation was that a site designer be engaged who was familiar with the problems of rugged terrain.

Planning From Within

Planning a twelve grade school from within was a new idea to these people, but they liked the concept and the end product resulted in one of the most functional, best designed schools in the world today. It is a multi-storied structure stair-stepped up the mountain-side taking full advantage of the difficult site. By pooling the know-how of the local staff with that of specialists in the planning and design field such as The Blurock Partnership and the site planners from Oregon, a jewel resulted.

Design Sketch, Rio

The school board at the suggestion of Vern Feiock, our planner in charge of the project, arranged to send some of their key faculty members to the San Francisco Bay area in California to learn more about newer concepts of teaching. Working with the superintendent, Gil Brown, and an enthusiastic board resulted in this becoming one of our more rewarding projects at that time.

UNIVERSITY OF ALASKA

The Ford Foundation furnished funds to the Educational Facilities Laboratories which in turn subsidized Stanford University to pass funds on to the Western Regional Center administered by the Stanford School Planning Laboratory in order to underwrite facilities planning projects that were worthy of support. In 1959 the University of Alaska, located five miles from Fairbanks, was the beneficiary of this roundabout procedure and received a $100,000.00 grant for planning new facilities. I was closely involved with the project.

For the university faculty, planning from within for the proposed major additional facilities on the campus was a new concept. The existing plant had for the most part been built with little thought of its ultimate use by those who would be teaching and doing research in the buildings. Our idea of "planning for use" met with some resistance from staff members and the common complaint of lack of time for this type of activity was expressed at practically every session. We also ran headlong into the spirit of the pioneer who was supposed to bull things through in the manner demonstrated in Alaska for years by lumbermen, miners and hunters.

Pioneering Spirit

That pioneering attitude became evident when I spent an evening at President Patty's home on the campus. It must have been nearly 60 degrees below zero that night; a fact verified as we watched a huge moose lumber across the lawn, his frozen breath surrounding him like the water vapor escaping from a steam locomotive. Evenings of that nature are conducive to staying indoors, and are called two or three dog nights—depending upon how many dogs a miner required to sleep with him to maintain a comfortable temperature under his blankets.

"Muskoxology"

In addition to the educational programming, we supervised the master planning of the 2,200 acre campus, and evaluated agriculture stations, a musk ox farm, the functional aspects of ice floes, and a cold weather research facility at Point Barrow.

Selling some of the main campus land had been under consideration, but we discouraged that and encouraged the purchase of additional acreage, and recommended that an additional campus be located in Anchorage.

The most gratifying part of participating in master planning of this nature comes with being a part of something that will influence the lives of students long after the study and its participants are forgotten. Most projects of this type are appreciated only years later when the work is recognized as the result of routine accommodation of anticipated natural growth.

On the University of Alaska project, however, the Regents of the University expressed their immediate recognition of the benefits that would ultimately be realized by presenting us with a resolution of appreciation.

BOARD OF REGENTS

Resolution of Appreciation

to

THE FORD FOUNDATION

and

THE STANFORD MASTER PLANNING GROUP

Whereas, Dr. James D. MacConnell, Director, Western Regional Center, Educational Facilities Laboratory, Stanford University, and his associates, including Dr. Glenn Kendall, President, Chico State College; Dr. Raymond C. Schneider, and Mr. Don Kenny have submitted to the Board of Regents of the University of Alaska a long-range "Master Program Development Plan" for the University of Alaska; and

Whereas, the aforementioned "Master Program Development Plan" is an excellent analysis of the problems and potentialities of higher education in Alaska and reflects long and painstaking effort on the part of the Director and his consultants; and

Whereas, the proposed "Master Program Development Plan" is recognized and accepted by the Board of Regents as a scholarly and practical approach to the development of a sound program of Instruction, Research, and Service for the State of Alaska and its public Land-Grant University; and

Whereas, Dr. James D. MacConnell and his associates, including Mr. Mario J. Ciampi, noted Architect and community planning authority, Mr. Lawrence Lackey, Architect and Urban Design Consultant, Mr. Don Knorr, Architect, and Mr. Paul W. Reiter, Associate Architect, have presented to the Board of Regents of the University of Alaska a well-conceived long-range "Master Campus Development Plan" for the University of Alaska based upon the educational needs and specifications set forth in the proposed "Master Program Development Plan"; and

Whereas, the "Master Campus Development Plan" is an expertly prepared, imaginative, and useful projection of basic information essential to the successful development of the facilities to meet the rapidly growing higher education demands being placed upon the University of Alaska; and

Whereas, the Ford Foundation through its substantial and generous financial support has made possible the Master Planning Studies that provide an exceedingly valuable guide for the future development of the University of Alaska; and

Whereas, the encouragement and backing of the Ford Foundation has resulted in an attractive and useful series of Project Reports and a Master Plan for Educational Program and Campus Development that is objective, unbiased, educationally acceptable, and possible of attainment;

Now, Therefore, be it resolved that the Board of Regents of the University of Alaska officially extends its sincere appreciation to the Ford Foundation for its truly significant contribution to the development of higher education in the State of Alaska, a contribution of very great worth to the people of all Alaska;

And, be it further resolved that the Board of Regents seize this occasion to acknowledge with deepest thanks the highly talented professional services of Dr. James D. MacConnell, Mr. Mario J. Ciampi, and their associates and consultants.

Inscribed in the official minutes of the October 20-22, 1960, Meeting of the Board

AMERICAN SAMOA

Planning *for* and designing educational facilities in American Samoa added a variety of new experiences to those we had already collected. Among them was instruction by educational television which was familiar to us as a supplementary teaching technique but not as a primary medium.

Map of American Samoa showing Tutuila and Manu'a islands, 60 miles apart, with elementary school and high school locations marked.

- Elementary School
- ▲ High School

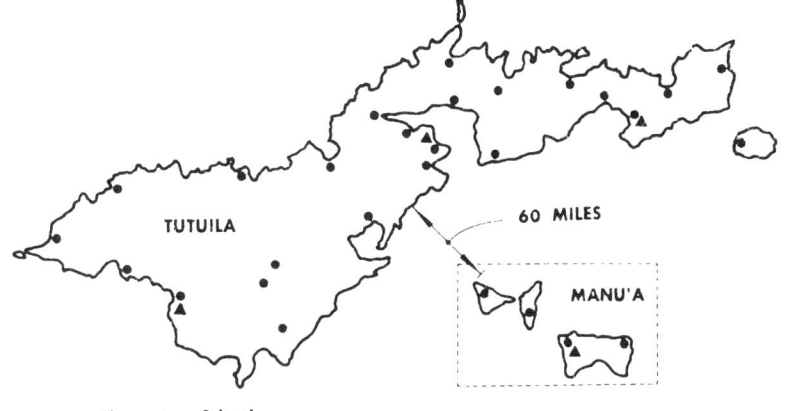

School locations planned

Recruiting teachers for the islands was difficult, but persuading them to stay after they were hired proved to be even more so. The peripatetic teachers were not alone; some of the pictures of the past governors displayed in the capitol building disclosed the fact that a couple had only stayed one day. The sixteen feet of rain per annum with the resultant excessive humidity may have been a factor. One visitor swore that after being there two weeks he felt gills emerging on his neck.

Instead of supplementing the teaching, a centralized Educational Television broadcasting network had been set up to supply the bulk of the curriculum in all the schools in the islands. In this manner, the effects of poorly trained teachers could be partially overcome, the lack of transportation could be negated for the moment, and through careful, but im-

Educational Television

aginative use, the educational television system could overcome the natural animosity toward all things foreign while uplifting the educational standards of 50,000 people.

New facilities were necessary to house the new Educational Television based educational program—grass huts simply would not do. We were there to assist in the development of new facilities. The planning team provided four services: 1) A master plan for secondary school facilities, 2) An analysis of existing facilities and a projection of future needs, 3) Educational specifications for four high schools with flexible, functional spaces for Educational Television, and 4) A furniture design for elementary youngsters.

The Solutions

One of the essentials for a successful educational program was the need to develop schools which would mean more to the Samoans than the American surplus buildings they had been accustomed to. The design of the new schools paralleled that of Samoan dwellings and integrated the old and the new. The buildings were aesthetically pleasing, functional, and sufficiently flexible to house the changes that will occur in the character of Samoan life and education.

I was directed by the Governor to select an architect with an international reputation to design the buildings in compliance with our program specifications. The firm of John Lyon Read was selected. Due to the lack of building materials in Samoa it was necessary to use treated redwood (to discourage termite damage) from California and tilt up concrete sidewalls for construction materials. Transporting 100 foot-long redwood logs by barge from San Francisco to Samoa was in itself an accomplishment.

People often make things worse when they try to get you out of an embarrassing situation. After completing a presentation and being complimented by many people, the president of the group said to me, "I think that is the best talk on education that I have ever heard." A teen-age boy standing behind her said, "I haven't heard many talks, but this was the worst one I ever heard." The lady turned to me and said in a highly indignant voice, "Don't pay any attention to him. He's an idiot. He just runs around repeating what he hears other people say."

Private Consulting at Stanford

I had been encouraged to believe that the difference between my Navy and Stanford salaries could be made up by doing consulting work. Actually my first year at Stanford yielded only fifty dollars in consulting revenue.

ODELL AND MacCONNELL

Dr. William Odell, former Superintendent of Schools in Oakland, California, had joined the staff at Stanford the same year I did. A full professor of education, Bill had also arranged for consulting time. He had the advantage of already being known and recognized in the state as a leader in the field of school administration.

It occurred to me that with my interest in planning and Professor Odell's established reputation, a two-man team approach to the consulting field would be mutually beneficial. Dr. Odell concurred and before long we were both able to supplement our incomes from Stanford so that it was possible for us both to approach our former standards of living.

Long Lasting

This relationship was long lasting, in spite of a number of occasions when we disagreed on how certain projects should be managed. At times I felt that Bill was the type of strong person who could make wrong seem right just by saying that it was. Not having experienced big city administration, I was constantly trying to convince him that school administration was the same regardless of the size of the district.

Although most people wondered how we worked so well together, we both realized that totally different philosophies and backgrounds made for a strong consulting team. We agreed that Santa Clara County, where Stanford was physically located, and adjoining San Mateo County primarily would be home base for School of Education sponsored intern projects. In all other areas, as private consultants we would compete with other college and university professors, who like us were assisting school districts and getting paid for it.

> *Be it known to*
>
> ## William R. Odell and James D. MacConnell
>
> *that we do hereby express our esteem and warm appreciation for those qualities of:*
>
> Excellence of LEADERSHIP in providing an effective program of administrative training, knowledge, and skill acquisition experiences
>
> Demonstration of CONSIDERATION in providing appropriate guidance and personal counsel leading toward realistic appraisal of professional objectives
>
> Readiness of SPONSORSHIP that satisfies the particular individual needs, be they financial, experiental or personal
>
> Warmth of FELLOWSHIP in sharing the joys and allaying frustrations attendant to graduate academic pursuits
>
> Those who have been participants in these associations look forward to the perpetuation of the spirit of the program as embodied by those qualities, and they offer with appreciation and devotion their continued support and assistance.
>
> *Signed*
>
> *Your Boys*
>
> Those interns and assistants of the decade 1950-1959

A Boost from "Time"

When *Time* magazine published an article on my interest and contribution in the planning field, school districts throughout the country wrote to us for assistance with their planning programs. Missoula, Montana, was one of the first schools to offer us a consulting contract. From this small, ten thousand dollar contract grew the largest educational consulting firm in the United States. Employing up to seventy-five educational consultants, we eventually completed over four hundred consulting projects throughout the world.

SAN MATEO JUNIOR COLLEGE

The first junior college board to approach us for assistance was from San Mateo, the county located between San Francisco and Santa Clara Counties. Together, the three counties make up the San Francisco peninsula. Although this junior college had been long established, its enrollment had grown only from 677 in 1929-30 to 1,174 in 1951-52 when we began our study.

With bulging elementary and secondary schools, most two-year community colleges were anticipating explosive growth. The San Mateo Board wanted to have its organization, curriculum and new sites and facilities ready to accommodate the boom when it arrived.

The philosophy of community colleges that they should be easily reachable by the community put a limit on the size of the campus, given the number of available sites. With these factors in mind, the potential parcels were identified and a site selection program adopted and priorities assigned.

The $1.00 Site

The largest potential site, Coyote Point, had been a U.S. Marine Corps base. The fact that it could be obtained for $1.00 added many complications. It soon became evident that the public favored something free, even if it didn't serve the purpose best.

The San Francisco Airport was also in the district and flight patterns led many takeoffs and landing over Coyote Point. I was concerned with the noise that the introduction of jet planes would have on this site in the future. In conferences airport officials assured me that jets would not be a problem in my lifetime. They must have anticipated my early demise, as shortly thereafter the jets took over.

The timely study resulted in today's San Mateo Community College. It is located on three campuses, Cañada, Skyline and San Mateo, and has an enrollment of over thirty thousand students.

A Complex Study

The San Mateo study made me realize that planning becomes much more complex at the college level. Making presentations to a board as sophisticated as that in San Mateo mandated employing the best demographic and research techniques available, as well as knowing the makeup of the citizenry in the listening audience as presentations were made.

I could not help but remember the story told about St. Peter's advice as he welcomed a new arrival through the Pearly Gates and informed him that he was to make a ten minute speech, and to quickly choose his subject. The newcomer announced that he was a survivor of the Galveston Flood and that he would like to talk about that. St. Peter responded favorably but warned him that Noah was in the audience.

Although we did many more studies of this nature, I always felt that this one was one of the most comprehensive that we ever did and have always been grateful for the opportunity to participate that was given to me and my associates by the San Mateo Junior College Board.

CLARK COUNTY, NEVADA

Clark County, Nevada, the southern-most county in Nevada, includes the cities of Las Vegas, Henderson, and Boulder City. Boulder City came into existence with the construction of Hoover Dam, later to be named Boulder Dam and finally renamed Hoover Dam. Henderson became the home of Stauffer Chemical Company in the West, and Las Vegas became known as the gambling center of the world.

As part of a state imposed school reorganization plan all local districts were consolidated into one unit in each county. The Clark County district was larger than the state of Rhode Island! There were indications that the newly organized district, under the direction of Superintendent Guild Gray and a seven-member board of education, was about to experience a population explosion.

The 20 Year Study

In 1955 the team of Odell and MacConnell was invited to make a study of the potential growth of the district and to advise the superintendent and board as to what steps to take if its assumptions were verified. This was the first study in which we had the opportunity to put our demographic projections into practice, and to be able to verify them shortly thereafter as thousands of newcomers became residents of the district.

The early days of the study brought us into contact with government agencies and with Governor and later Senator Paul Laxalt. We also met many private businessmen including those from airlines, telephone and gas companies, casinos and other enterprises. The first job we faced was to convince ourselves, and then the board and superintendent, that the board's growth expectations were indeed justified. The effect on the community of the report to the board was not too dissimilar to the rumblings from the underground atomic tests that were being conducted some seventy miles away.

Our initial recommendation was for the immediate selection and purchase of over one hundred elementary and secondary school sites and to begin initial planning for school facilities that could accommodate a minimum of 85,000 students by 1985, some thirty years hence.

Buy 100 Sites

The recommendation might have been received better had representatives of the press not been at the Board meeting where it was presented. The subsequent uncomplimentary headlines in the local papers could hardly go unnoticed. "Professors Go Home," was one I remember and the fine print that followed was even less gratifying. Some phone calls by local citizens to Stanford suggested that I not be allowed to leave the Campus. Who would have guessed then that, some fifteen years later, an apology would be printed, in small print on the back page of the paper, to the effect that the professors had done a commendable job.

Thirty years later, the school enrollment in Clark County was 86,131. Over $300,000,000.00 worth of schools have been planned for, designed and built. Land values have quadrupled or more since 1955. School sites that were purchased for from $250 to $2,000 per acre are now properly located for growth and if purchased today, would represent millions of dollars in additional expense. It has been estimated by land appraisers that the advance planning and purchasing resulted in the equivalent of at least six secondary schools, totally equipped, being presented to the district without cost.

One of the great satisfactions that comes with consulting is to live long enough to see a project of this nature culminate. The original consulting agreement could be terminated with a sixty-day notice by either party. The termination clause was finally exercised twenty years later in 1975, when the student

It's Great to be Right

enrollment in Clark County had peaked and the local staff was sufficient in number to adequately carry on the planning responsibilities of the district.

In all ways the Clark County study was a gratifying project. It was of a size and scope to provide many learning experiences for Stanford graduate students majoring in school administration. One of them, Dr. Kenny Guinn, later spent nine years as Superintendent of Clark County Schools, and is currently President of the Nevada Savings and Loan and the Southwest Gas Company in Las Vegas.

Gallup's Advice Realized

In addition to helping the school district improve its long and short range educational and facilities planning, the Clark County experience gave me an opportunity to seriously apply the advice given by Mr. Gallup at the Michigan State Department of Education so many years before, that "You can seldom reach the financial level that will satisfy you unless you supplement your salary by wise long term investments."

Las Vegas had the appearance to me of a city that had expansion potential in practically every direction. Although Clark County was surrounded mostly by land owned by the Federal government, there were 110 sections that were privately owned, and constituted an island that eventually would be needed for both houses and commercial buildings.

The possibility of forming small syndicates to purchase some parcels of land with low down-payments appeared to be a sound investment. The outlying acreage was the most appropriate not only because it was less expensive than that closer to Las Vegas, but because it would avoid any charge of conflict of interest on my part to the citizens of the school district. As a precaution, however, I met with the school board and we agreed that should there ever be a parcel of land that we owned that the board wanted for school purposes, the school district could purchase it from us at our cost.

Over the years a number of small land purchase syndicates were formed with the guidance of Robert Lewis, an attorney who tended to

the legal aspects. Although the land payments seemed to keep June and me broke, the gratification of increased security was always present. My dreams from childhood had been not only to own a Rickenbacker automobile but to be in a position to help my parents and others close to me to have things in life that they deserved but could not afford. As I look back I am certain that some of the decisions I made on investments such as the Las Vegas property resulted in my being able in a small way to fulfill some of my dreams. I never did get the Rickenbacker, though.

MID MICHIGAN COMMUNITY COLLEGE

In considering undertaking a consulting project, we view the assistance we can offer in the light of whether or not we can make a profit by helping to identify and solve problems. Profit is not an unreasonable motive, but I am convinced that at times we must keep in touch with aspects of a project that will pay off in satisfaction rather than dollars.

Mid Michigan Community College, located in Gladwin county where I spent ten years as an educator, was such a project. I have taken a keen interest in its progress since its inception in 1962 to its stature today as a mature institution serving the needs of five school districts. No doubt my interest in rural youth and the fact that I knew the area, encouraged me to lend a helping hand when such action seemed appropriate.

A Long Term Relationship

A trip to the state capital, with the Community College president was made to strengthen the hand of the college in pleading for a five-hundred-acre site. A smaller plot that had been approved would have met the needs of the early generation of students, but would have hindered the promotion of additional projects that would require additional space in the future. Helping develop the program of the college and advise the president and board of trustees on facilities, as well as appearing at graduation and other programs, have been stimulating experiences for me.

In the past few years I have been in a position to give the school some limited financial assistance earmarked for the development of a community center. The scarcity of school funds in Michigan delayed this project for many years but it may be back on track soon. When it is built the youth and adults in the community will be able to enjoy or to learn something that might not have been possible without that little boost.

The world is built on faith. If those early doubters who said that there would never be more than a hundred students attending Mid Michigan Community College could return today and see the thousands of youth, adults and senior citizens now enrolled, they rightly would be amazed.

ENTER DMR
The consulting team of Odell and MacConnell soon outgrew quarters in the School of Education and took space in a portion of the campus reserved for private business and professional offices. As consulting contracts increased we employed former graduate students to implement many of the planning projects.

By 1967 Dr. Odell was experiencing some health problems and was becoming less enthusiastic about our joint consulting program. He was not philosophically a team man, and often questioned the ability of young people to carry responsibility and make decisions.

We decided to go our separate ways. Donald Davis and Ira Ralston, two former graduate students, would become my partners in a corporation named DMR—Davis, MacConnell and Ralston. Dr. Odell's interest in the former partnership was purchased over a five-year period. Donald Davis was named prsident of the new company since my being a professor at Stanford precluded accepting that position.

Australia
In 1967 I was invited by the Australian government to visit that country on a lecture tour to acquaint school people, architects and engineers with the advantages of functional planning of educational facilities. At that time Australia had provided amounts of federal funds for building new and rehabilitating existing educational facilities. I spoke to and made visual presentations to groups across the entire country from Sydney to Perth, as well as in the state of Tasmania.

While in the Australian capital of Canberra, I was asked to attend a school board meeting to help mitigate a dispute over a potential secondary school that was in its early planning stages. I was introduced to the board members by a Federal Office of Education employee as an expert in planning educational facilities from the States. That introduction alone probably made me suspect. The president of the board, who looked like a self-made educator, opened her remarks by asking, "Doctor MacConnell, are you in favor of one or two-story buildings?" I responded by saying that there were many factors that would have to be considered such as curriculum, cost of acreage, and so on, before the number of stories could be determined. The president then said that she had expected such evasive answers when she heard that I was a specialist from the United States. I responded by thanking the Board for the valuable time that I had taken from their meeting and departed.

The island state of Tasmania was in the early phase of its planning, a situation which presented the greatest opportunity for a major contribution. The Tasmanian College of Advanced Education had recently acquired a two-hundred acre site for a new facility, and had employed some young architects and assigned them to buildings that had already been designed when I arrived on the scene.

Reviewing the plans, I realized that most of the buildings, when completed, would be inadequate to house the programs for which they were designed. The following meeting with the board was one of the most uncomfortable I have ever attended. The president of the board let it be known that one million dollars had already been spent, and to learn that those funds were spent to design inadequate buildings disturbed him, to say the least. His opening statement was, "I told you monkeys that we were going at this planning backwards."

The upshot of the meeting was that DMR and the Blurock Partnership, an architectural firm in Newport Beach, California, with whom we had worked, were employed to start from scratch and re-do the project, providing detailed educational specifications and a master plan that would site the buildings in closer proximity. It became evident to everyone that a small college need not use its two-hundred acre site all at once.

Tasmania

Project Re-do

After the facilities were completed, one of the DMR consultants was employed by the college board to be the new president of the college.

DMR WESTINGHOUSE

By the fall of 1969 DMR was recognized as an educational consulting firm of stature. It employed between fifty and seventy-five full-time consultants and was working for school districts, colleges and universities throughout the United States as well as in many locations overseas.

That was the era when all types of educational companies were being acquired by large corporations that wanted to get into the education business which was booming because of increased school enrollments. The use of more sophisticated equipment by students at all levels led some manufacturing companies to acquire educational arms.

Within a period of two months five companies approached us to sell out to them. Among them were Hauserman, Lytton, and the Westinghouse Learning Corporation which was headquartered in New York. Although that ultimately proved to be the exact time when companies of that nature should have been selling off such divisions because of the pending recession, a deal was consummated and within weeks we were proud owners of Westinghouse common stock and became known as DMR, a Division of Westinghouse Learning Corporation.

As the months passed it became clear that although the Westinghouse Learning Corporation had spent some twenty mil-

JDM; 1968

160

lion dollars on its instructional program called PLAN, and had also ventured into other educational enterprises, its expertise was not in educational planning. When our backlog of planning projects hovered around six weeks, and the Westinghouse manufacturing backlog more like six years, we realized that we were in a different world and that the Learning Corporation probably was not going to become a giant in the education field. The experience demonstrated to me that the skills needed to succeed in managing the manufacture of "things" are much different from those needed to manage educators and operate educational processes. The bottom line, not the bottom child, was the determining factor.

Within two years, our organization, as well as others that had become a part of the Westinghouse Learning Corporation family, was in shambles. The result was that the dedicated, competent educators who had constituted DMR were scattered to the four winds. I remained a consultant to the Learning Corporation until 1980, primarily to help them wind down the program, and to try to determine for my own satisfaction why the venture was a failure.

The Break-up

I now feel that the organization was improperly set up. When burdened with a large corporate overhead, a small division cannot survive to become a profit center. I am also convinced that educational consulting has to be highly personalized, and for the most part, requires that service have a high priority, which often minimizes profit.

Having been involved in numerous business partnerships I have come to feel that some partnerships are more equal than others. I am reminded of the pig and the chicken who were walking down the street and saw a restaurant sign that read, "Ham and Eggs". "See," said the chicken, "we are partners!" "Yes," said the pig. "One day's work for you—but for me the supreme sacrifice!"

A friend was questioning his associate as to the success of a recent trip to Las Vegas and was given the following response: "I drove to Vegas in my $25,000 Lincoln Continental and came home in a $400,000 Greyhound bus."

Beyond the Farm—Retirement Aftermath

May 26, 1973 was my sixty-fifth birthday as well as the day that Stanford declared me intellectually dead. I was not alone in this predicament as most other universities then retired their employees at that age. I have been told that we inherited that arbitrary cut-off date from the Romans, and I suspect it probably has to do with earlier times when men had a shorter life span.

Regardless of where it originated, I found it difficult to accept the fact that my professional life was being terminated. As a person in love with his profession who had looked forward to going to work every day, retirement came as a shock to me. Twenty-five great years at Stanford had passed and suddenly I was feeling sorry for myself and wondering what was ahead.

Retirement   My colleague and professional partner Bill Odell had passed away a few months before and I realized that while some people get tired of work, I would reach a point within weeks when I would be tired of retirement. I had done some reading about "preparing for retirement," which was mostly hints about selecting hobbies, doing volunteer work, traveling and so on. I had already belonged to the Palo Alto Hills Country Club and June and I were playing some golf. But I had always been among the winners in my profession, so I guess that being a consistent loser with my golfing partners depressed me and provided more time to regret the fact that I was no longer in a position to make some kind of a contribution. Being a volunteer didn't really appeal to me. My philosophy had always been that you got paid for doing work, and if I wanted to give the money away—that was my business.

The travel bit was out. From the time I left the Beaverton superintendency I had been traveling. Being a restless soul, I enjoyed it, but I was quick to realize that traveling is expensive, and that the travel brochures were not written and illustrated by shrinking violets. I had also experienced extreme boredom on my professional travels once the work was done and I was forced to enjoy myself while awaiting transportation home, or on to another project.

Most of my colleagues who had retired were seemingly enjoying themselves. When I would mention that I would like to get some part-time consulting work, however, they would usually ask to be counted in if I should start an educational consulting company. This did little to allay my fears that there really were only a few happy retirees who had been active in the field of education.

My retirement party on the evening of my birthday was a gala affair. Even the University had a representative there. I couldn't determine whether they were more pleased that I would be out of their hair, or really appreciated what I had contributed since joining the staff in 1948. At that point it didn't matter. I did have my suspicions, however, when I called into the School Planning Lab the following week to find the name had been changed to "Administration and Policy Analysis."

I felt I was in the same position as the Midwest college coach who had been nicknamed by the college students and alumni as "Winning Joe." He had just completed fifty consecutive winning basketball games when the president called him into his office and presented him with a lifetime appointment accompanied by a substantial raise in pay. The next three years, however, he lost every game. When he again was summoned to the president's office, he was declared legally dead and fired.

There were hundreds of people at the retirement party, including my brother John and his wife Carol, my sister Isabelle, President Eugene Gillaspy and his wife Gertrude and Doug Hall, the president of the board of trustees and his wife Sally, from Mid Michigan Community College. I saw former graduate students I had not seen since they graduated, many of whom had accepted positions away from the Bay Area but had kept in touch. There were many with whom I was still working such as Don and Beverly Davis and others

A Gala Affair

who had taken it upon themselves, along with June, to sponsor this most special occasion for me.

It pleased me no end to note that many who came were from a variety of disciplines such as attorneys, bankers, furniture manufacturers, architects, educators and even some friends I usually met for breakfast at the Lemon Tree, a coffee shop that I frequented en route to Stanford.

STEPPING ASIDE

I suppose it was time that I stepped aside. The training of school administrators was changing. Administrators no longer were the dominant decision makers in the schools, or even in colleges and universities. Faculty members and students were choosing up sides against the administrators and a new vocabulary was coming into prominence including such words as arbitration, student rights, faculty rights, strikes and so on. I am not saying that this is wrong, but it definitely was occupying more of an administrator's time and required training in new skills.

Theoretically, I had always been a great believer in change. It was easy to tell students in my lectures on "social interpretation" that, unlike their grandparents, they no doubt would be working in three or four different careers before they reached retirement age. But I had stayed with one career and now was entering retirement with mixed emotions.

Filling Time

After considering our options, it appeared to June and me that a motor home could satisfy our travel needs. The home away from home, an ocean view one time followed by a trip to the mountains the next time, seemed a better alternative than a cottage in a static location. Additionally, a colleague, Dudley Boice and his wife and we had purchased a condominium on Maui, in the Hawaiian Islands which we rented out when not occupying it. It proved to be an enjoyable place to visit when time permitted, which became increasingly infrequent so we sold it last year. We made a trip in the motor home to the East Coast with June's parents in the fall of 1974, and although I felt that I was slowly adjusting to this new way of living, things apparently were not as good mentally and physically as I imagined. I had been taking some medication for high blood pressure which apparently was the cause for some of the problems that followed.

I had learned to sublimate the idea that debt was the result of poor management, and I knew very well that one could owe money and yet be respectable. In fact, with inflation, one's wealth was often measured by the amount of money one could borrow. As one of my colleagues told me, "Bev and I must be wealthy, for we have never owed so much money in our lives."

Early in 1975, while on a motor home vacation in San Diego, my whole world fell apart. Realizing that I owed more money than I thought that I would ever be worth, all of a sudden I felt certain that it was all coming due. After returning from the trip, I saw an attorney about filing bankruptcy papers which he talked me out of. I didn't want to see anyone or go anyplace. It didn't take long to realize that I was having a nervous breakdown.

Collapse

Up until then I had always made light of people who had mental problems of this type. It had always seemed to be something that people went through only if they could afford it. But when my doctor recommended that I see a psychiatrist, I gladly consented. I remarked that I would like to meet one, for I had spent a good part of my adult life poking fun at them. I felt like the man who had been taken to a psychiatrist because he thought that he was a dog and insisted on chasing automobiles. When asked how long he had felt that way, he answered, "Ever since I was a pup."

After a couple of sessions the psychiatrist and I began to explore the probable reasons for my condition. It didn't take long for the doctor to come to the conclusion that my trouble stemmed from two major sources—not being as important as I once was, and using a specific high blood pressure pill that caused side effects, one of them being deep depression.

I had cancelled a number of presentations during the previous two months, but a change in medication coinciding

Up Again

with a call to assist in a planning project in Cairo restored my confidence in myself and in three weeks I was heading for Egypt. Working with a Washington, D.C. architect and the board of education of the American University in Cairo put me back on track and resulted in another successful educator-architect joint venture.

June accompanied me on this trip. She felt that the trip would do me good, but I was reminded of a community in Northern Michigan that would often take up a collection for an ailing citizen in the dead of winter and send him or her to Long Beach, California, for a break from the cold and snow. The recipients usually returned in a few weeks with a new lease on life. One lucky candidate left home on January 2. Unlike the others, he worsened in February, and in early March passed away. As his family gathered around him in the casket, all dressed up and wearing a deep tan, his wife was heard to remark, "Doesn't he look wonderful? I think the trip did him a lot of good."

CAIRO

The trip was not financially productive. Consultants could not be paid in American dollars, so the remuneration was taken care of by paying our air fare and other expenses, plus furnishing additional funds for local purchases in Cairo. This resulted in our purchasing items we could well have done without, but it was fun.

While there, I met Jamine, a Saudi Arabian who was impressed with what I was doing in Cairo. He invited me to come directly from Egypt to Riyadh, Saudi Arabia. As I interpreted his business card, he was Superintendent of Schools in Riyadh. In fact he was really the headmaster of a struggling school there.

Arranging for a visa in Cairo to enter Saudi Arabia proved to be the trick of the week. When I was finally authorized to travel June returned to California. I purchased a first class air ticket to Saudi Arabia, since the word from the travel agency was that at that late date there were no coach tickets available. When it turned out that no more than a couple dozen coach seats were occupied in a plane that provided for over a hundred, I began to wonder whether the travel agent or I should have been counting the vacant seats.

Riyadh

There were two stops between Cairo and Riyadh. These stops provided my first introduction to the Saudi way of life. It was interesting to watch the Saudi men getting off the plane carrying little rugs that they placed on the floor of the terminal and then faced Mecca with only their knees and elbows touching the rug while they recited their ritual prayers.

My arrival at Riyadh was a disaster. Not only did I land in the midst of a heavy rainstorm, but the Saudi who had invited me was not there to meet me. I had no Saudi money to pay the children who grabbed my bags and headed for a cab. To try to explain to a non-English speaking cab driver that you have no money with which to pay the boys, and that you have no hotel reservation, and further that you will not be able to pay him until you get some Saudi money, proved to be both difficult and embarrassing.

Apparently my plight was not uncommon, for the cab driver paid the helpers, took me to the hotel and waited at the desk for me to exchange dollars for rials. I was taken to my room by an English-speaking Lebanese bell boy and found that the air conditioning consisted of a slowly moving fan in the ceiling. By morning the bed sheets were soaking and the temperature was hovering around 120 degrees.

Where's Jamine?

When the desk attendant, another English-speaking Lebanese, looked at the business card of Jamine who was to meet me, he said, "Oh yes, I know him, but you won't be able to see him for a couple of days." Then he explained that it was Thursday morning and that Saudis prayed Thursdays and Fridays, which was their weekend. When I asked what I could do to pass the time for the next two days, he suggested that I go to an execution which was scheduled for the next day. There would be many people there, and "the hotel would pack me a lunch."

I told him not to bother, but that I would appreciate his securing me a cab as I was determined to try to make contact with the man who was to meet me. The trip to Jamine's home was an experience in itself. Saudis don't do much common labor, but they love to drive cabs, and fast!

Jamine		Jamine was surprised to see me and said that he had not received my telegram. His home was beautiful inside and his wife, an Egyptian girl, was equally beautiful. After a short talk about the type of help he needed, we set up a schedule to follow after the weekend. Then he suggested we go out to dinner. That was the last time I saw his wife and was my introduction to the Saudi practice of excluding women from events of that nature.

The next few days proved to be interesting but somewhat disastrous, professionally. Jamine didn't seem to have the backing of his board, nor did they appear to understand why I was there.

In the United States at that time we were building schools that were quite open, encouraging team teaching, and individual and small group instruction. But after making my presentation, I realized that I was definitely not going to change the structure or teaching methodology of that Saudi Arabian school system.

Jamine took me to see the site where the proposed school was to be located, replacing several portable buildings which were currently housing classes. As we stood on the site in a fierce sand storm I felt that I was watching at least two school sites blow by. I was beginning to realize that, although things had gone well in Egypt, there was no guarantee that the same experience was going to be repeated in Saudi Arabia. The following day I was pleased to be one of the passengers on the plane to New York and on to San Francisco.

NE/SA		While attending the American Association of School Administrators annual meeting in Atlanta, Georgia, in February, 1976, Bob Ingraham, a former graduate student and colleague of mine, introduced me to Pat Howard. She was executive secretary of NE/SA, the organization representing the English-speaking schools in the Near East and Southeast Asia. Bob had told her I had been speaking before school administrators and teachers throughout the world and would be a likely candidate to speak at the November, 1977 NE/SA meeting that was to take place on the Greek island of Rhodes. After my interview with her, it was mutually agreed that I would attend the conference and speak at two general sessions as well as conduct two seminars.

I spent a considerable amount of time preparing for the meeting. Having had a successful experience in Egypt and an unsuccessful one in Saudi Arabia, I looked for an opportunity to make another visit to that part of the world.

SABBATICAL TRAVELS

The visit to Egypt and Saudi Arabia and the upcoming trip to Rhodes had not been my first encounter with that part of the world. I had been there some fifteen years previously while on my second sabbatical from Stanford.

On that trip June and I had left San Francisco and flying in a westerly direction circumnavigated the globe in some three months time and definitely demonstrating to June's satisfaction that Columbus was right; the world is round.

Visiting Schools

We visited schools in Japan, Indonesia, India, Greece, Turkey, Lebanon, Israel and Egypt and other countries in between. We were looking for evidences of functional design and space planning of schools which would help our work in the School Planning Lab.

We had been exposed to pockets of poverty in the United States but they were nothing compared to what we saw on that trip. In many of the countries it was an overwhelming problem—one which education and family planning must attack.

On our previous sabbatical June and I had visited schools in Mexico as a guest of the Mexico City director of school planning and saw at first hand a problem associated with new school construction that we hadn't covered in our classes. Often before a new school could be occupied by students it was taken over by squatters—families with no place to live who would move bodily and in large numbers into the vacant school building.

Beyond the Farm—Consulting Overseas

Traveling from San Francisco to New York to Athens and then to the island of Rhodes for the meeting of NE/SA, the organization of English-speaking schools in the Near East and Southeast Asia, I found myself among old acquaintances who had left the states to practice their profession in another part of the world. Twelve of my former students and colleagues were in attendance, one of whom was Dr. Edwin Read who had recently been appointed Director of Education in the Eastern Province of Saudi Arabia by the Arab American Oil Company (ARAMCO). In that position he had educational responsibility for both the expatriate schools attended by children of American employees of ARAMCO and the Saudi Arabian schools attended by children of Saudi employees of ARAMCO.

ARAMCO—EXPATRIATE SCHOOLS

After my presentations Dr. Read invited me to go to Saudi Arabia in January, 1978 to consult on planning for a proposed series of expatriate schools. Introducing the concept of master planning and educational specifications would be a challenge. At the time, "master planning" there consisted of supplying a portable classroom to house the latest thirty students who had arrived. The continuing added enrollment was caused by increased activity in oil and related industries.

In the subsequent meetings in Saudi Arabia it was possible to prove that planning not only would save money, but would also impose order on that rapidly expanding school system. Teachers were enthusiastic about the prospect of participating in grade and subject matter discussions that could result in bringing functional facilities to the expatriate schools of Saudi Arabia.

Dhahran

The meetings took place in Dhahran, ARAMCO's headquarters city, where some four thousand expatriate students attended elementary and junior high school. Additionally, there were a number of schools located in outlying areas. The dedication of the teachers in attending the meetings impressed me, for women there are not permitted to drive automobiles and it was necessary for them to make the uncomfortable trip in school buses.

Despite the positive attitudes of the teachers, the six weeks spent in Saudi Arabia were frustrating. Although I was being paid by ARAMCO, I was in Dhahran as an educational consultant to a large architectural firm, 3D International. The firm didn't know for sure what I was supposed to be doing since my mission there was "planning *for* schools" while personnel working for 3D International were "planning schools." In fact, my job was to prepare programs and educational specifications, while theirs was to design facilities to accommodate those programs.

I was informed that since their schedule was so tight, there would not be time to prepare educational specifications or programs and that it would be helpful if I could look over their architects' shoulders and tell them whether or not their designs were acceptable. This definitely was not what I had come to Saudi Arabia to do, and yet I couldn't figure a way out of the predicament.

Frustration

Being a believer in working and getting paid for it, or getting out of the picture, I approached the business manager of the expatriate schools, expressed my disappointment in the situation, and suggested that I should call it quits and leave for home. Then he asked me a question that got my attention, "Can you make $500.00 a day in Palo Alto?" I was quick to realize that I had better find a way to make an educational contribution. I knew that it could be done, but I just wasn't sure how.

A solution appeared when I arranged to be invited to an ARAMCO meeting where engineering studies were being discussed. The studies involved making the school facilities more functional and planning for some central core areas around which classrooms could be clustered. The project was challenging because there was an apparent need for different sized facilities varying from a three-room school to a grade or junior high school of considerable size. I sold the

Functional Planning

engineers on the idea that such a project was right up my alley and was asked to submit a proposal to that division of ARAMCO. This I did and later in the summer received a contract.

A New Team

The sales presentation had been successful, and now the task was to make a significant contribution to that group. There were some problems in this regard. My consulting firm, James D. MacConnell and Associates, Inc., was in need of some skilled associates, for I basically was a one-man show. I called in two of my former graduate students and associates, Howard Sagehorn and William Meadville, who had teamed up to form a consulting group after the demise of the DMR division of Westinghouse Learning Corporation. As it turned out, their recent hands-on planning experience along with my selling and interpreting ability made for a team that proved to be very functional. We moved to the penthouse floor of Five Palo Alto Square in the Stanford Industrial Park in Palo Alto, California, out of which we are currently operating.

We developed a system of "do it yourself educational specifications" which made it possible for an architect or engineer and an educator to knowledgeably plan for a facility that could accommodate practically any size group of students anywhere in the desert or in a small village. The time of construction or the exact place were of little concern. Later we were asked to help plan for some sizeable facilities at Abqaiq and Ras Tanura, and for an educational park and some renovation work in Dhahran.

At Times It Wasn't Easy

With this start, our presence in Saudi Arabia was recognized. Soon we were asked to assist with the preparation of planning for the ARAMCO-built government schools. These were schools being planned for Saudi students whose parents were employees of ARAMCO. We also assisted in the planning of a new private Muslim school.

One particular meeting in the early sessions with the ARAMCO engineers ended in near disaster when one of the more verbal engineers informed me that our approach was wrong. He said that he had been building schools for the Saudis for years and knew exactly what they needed.

He further expounded on the subject by accusing me of being unfair to the director by attempting to lead him down a primrose path and wasting ARAMCO money.

A meeting with Dr. Read resulted in removing that obstruction and eventually selling the concept that schools were for youth and not for engineers.

Situations of this type are common in dealing with people who are threatened by the introduction of unfamiliar concepts. As these situations arise I tend to follow the philosophy of the sparrow that was lying on its back with its feet in the air as an Arabian horseman approached. He questioned the sparrow as to its motives. The response was, "Haven't you heard that the sky is falling in today?" "What can those little legs and feet do to prevent such a crisis?" asked the horseman, to which the little sparrow replied, "One does what one can."

Girls' Multi-purpose/Prayer Room

ARAMCO-BUILT GOVERNMENT SCHOOLS

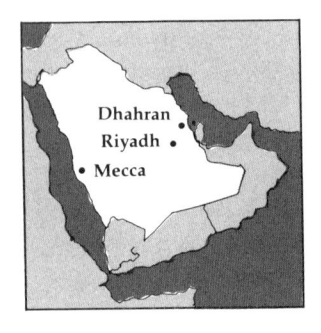

Consulting for the expatriate schools and then for the ARAMCO-built government schools was as different as day is from night. The only constant was that both were run by Dr. Edwin Read, Director of Education for both systems. The expatriate schools were under the direction of a superintendent of co-educational schools, with a school organization similar to that in the United States. The Saudi schools were under the auspices of two Directors General who were each responsible for a large number of schools and their principals. The Saudi schools were also segregated by sex. The shaykh, Dr. Said Abo Aali was Director-General responsible for the boys schools and reported to his superior, the Minister of Education in Riyadh, while his counterpart, Shaykh Nasir al Musaynid who directed the girls' schools, was a religious leader reporting to the Presidency of Girls' Education. Although these shaykhs were not members of the royal family, they held key positions and were recognized leaders in the Saudi educational system.

My colleague, Howard Sagehorn, Dr. Read and I made the initial call on the shaykhs. Dr. Read had had a good relationship with them for quite some time, and he was now proposing that our team help them to create a new generation of schools that would better serve the Saudi youth.

Meeting these gentlemen was intriguing. I have observed well-appointed offices, but few have come up to the level of those. We were also introduced to the social amenities of the Saudi culture. In our society when we schedule a meeting we immediately get to the business at hand. In contrast, the first half-hour and often at interludes during longer sessions, the Saudis serve a variety of non-alcoholic drinks usually starting with a cardamom-flavored coffee in small cups without handles followed by sweet tea in small glass mugs.

Opportunity

Our consulting opportunity was especially timely because of the magnitude of the school building program being faced in the Eastern Province. The increased focus on girls' schools, due to the demand of the government that every child attend school, added momentum to this large-scale program.

Although we had some doubt that we would be permitted to help, we were welcomed with open arms and offered the assistance of decision-makers on the staff in explaining the ramifications of the Saudi educational system. From the beginning we made it very clear that we were not there to change the curriculum, but to plan for facilities that would best accommodate present and future school activities.

In the boys' schools, while the students were Saudis for the most part, their teachers were not. They came from other Arab-speaking countries and included Egyptians, Sudanese and Palestinians. Some English was spoken or understood by the educators with whom we worked but the language barrier was a communication factor. The result was longer meetings than would have been necessary had we been communicating with fluent English speaking groups. We were grateful that the Saudi interpreters, for the most part Palestinians and Egyptians, did an excellent job in explaining not only what was being taught, but why.

Unlike the United States, where we are concerned with maintaining the separation of church and state, in Saudi Arabia religion is a key element in the curriculum. Space for prayer as well as space for teaching students how to pray is a primary requirement in space planning there. Orienting all the prayer areas to face Mecca is a must when planning facilities. A discussion as to whether to use Eastern or Western style toilets also took its toll in time.

Although many schools had been built in the past, especially boys' schools, little thought had been given to future curriculum changes that would require different spaces than those in use today. An expanding physical education program for the girls, for example, which might someday include basketball, caused us to encourage higher ceilings in the activity corners. We added conduits for electric typewriters, provided for computers, and suggested many other items that caused spirited discussions.

Change

The weather was certainly a factor to be considered. Although the temperature in Saudi Arabia often reaches 120 degrees, it is not a country that is unfamiliar with cold

Boys' Multi-purpose/Prayer room

weather. Theirs is not the Alaskan nor even the Midwestern cold, but it is cold enough to require heat in addition to air conditioning. The experience we had had in Clark County, Nevada, and with the SCSD project at Stanford, helped in planning with our architectural design consultant to provide facilities that would not only accommodate the current and future curriculum but would also be at home in the desert.

Finis   Nearly all school systems are handicapped by lack of funds in every area, from curriculum through completed facilities. This was not true in Saudi Arabia. They did not believe in wasting money, but there was evidence at every turn that they were willing to expend an appropriate share of their wealth in order to educate their youth.

In 1986 we completed our work in Saudi Arabia. The contribution of our team was major, for we planned the prototypes that would serve as the blueprints, with necessary alterations, for the buildings that would be built today and for years into the future.

There are some twenty-five projects now completed counting the expatriate ARAMCO-built Government Schools. They represent an expenditure of approximately a billion dollars and demonstrate a dedication of the Kingdom of Saudi Arabia to the future of the country.

Council of Educational Facility Planners, International
PLANNER OF THE YEAR – 1979

Dr. Moehlman would have been pleased—and surprised!

JAMES D. MacCONNELL

For exceptionally outstanding service to the profession through the creation and operation of the world-recognized Stanford School Planning Laboratory.

– presented October 31, 1979
Baltimore, Maryland

ITALY—FIVE NEW HIGH SCHOOLS

On November 23, 1980, a severe earthquake struck the southern part of Italy. The quake registerd 6.8 on the Richter Scale and was characterized as the most devastating disaster to strike Western Europe since World War II. The stricken area of approximately 10,000 square miles extended from Naples to Potenza. The cities of Naples, Salerno, Potenza and Avellino were damaged, and outside these urban centers 356 towns and villages, out of a total of 570, were damaged by the initial shock and its numerous aftershocks. Some towns and villages, in whole or in part, were simply flattened.

Earthquake Damage

The quake killed approximately 3,000 people and injured 7,700. Living quarters for 300,000 people were destroyed. Roughly 100,000 structures such as schools, houses and public buildings were damaged or demolished.

Following the quake, the U.S. Agency for International Development appropriated funds to assist the Italian government in the massive rebuilding effort. As one of the architects employed to design six new high schools in a portion of the devastated area, The Blurock Partnership enlisted our services in developing educational specifications for the new buildings.

The subsequent work in Italy was challenging. The opportunity to help the local school people and citizens in the towns of Nocera, Siano, Buccino, Muro Lucano, Picerno and Rionero in the provinces of Salerno and Potenza rethink their desired school program without the strictures of existing buildings was most rewarding.

New Approaches

Normally Italian high schools were devoted exclusively to only one program of study, such as classics, languages, sciences, business, teacher preparation, minerology, agriculture or technical studies. Our educational specifications and facilities recommendations were planned so as to offer two disciplines in each school. The approach provided greater opportunities for the students and anticipated the reform wherein all high school students would share a common educational experience during their first two years.

The required subjects in the academic and specialized areas were spelled out in the "Programmi Scholastici Pirola" curriculum guides. By careful planning and utilization of space for traditional activities, additional spaces were provided for the potential reformed curriculum and to care for youth and community activities that were stressed as essential by those we interviewed. The desire on the part of the young community leaders to see the school centers emerge as formal and informal educational centers was seriously dealt with in our planning.

Materie o gruppi di materie	BIENNIO classi I	II	Materie e gruppi di materie obbligatorie e per tutti	TRIENNIO classi III	IV	V
Religione	1	1	Religione	1	1	1
Italiano (s. e o.)	4	4	Lingua e lettere Italiane (s. e o.)	4	4	4
Latino (s. e o.)	3	3	Storia dell'arte (o.)	1	1	1
Storia dell'arte (o.)	1	1	Storia e Educazione Civica (o.)	2	2	2
Storia, Educazione Civica e Geografia (o.)	3	3	Filosofia, Psicologia e Sociologia (o.)	3	3	3
Prima lingua straniera (s. e o.)	5	5	Prima lingua straniera (s. e o.)	5	5	5
Seconda lingua straniera (s. e o.)	6	6	Seconda lingua straniera (s. e o.)	5	5	5
Matematica (o.) - Fisica (o.)	3	3	Matematica (o.) e Fisica (o.)	3	3	3
Educazione Fisica (p.)	2	2	Scienze Naturali e Geografia Generale ed Economica (o.)	2	2	2
	28	28	Educazione Fisica (p.)	2	2	2
				28	28	28

Classical High School Program

Those of us who struggle to be articulate in one language are humbled when we meet people throughout the world who not only speak fluent English but are also conversant in many other languages. Our Italian partners on the Italian project, architects Alberto Izzo and Camillo Gubitosi were so gifted and were responsible for our final report in both Italian and English.

Programmi Scolastici
In Italia, i programmi scolastici per i licei sono organizzati in specializzazioni o indirizzi. Il preciso programma per ogni indirizzo e' fornito dai programmi scolastici ufficiali governativi. Normalmente i licei Italiani offrono un solo corso di studio o indirizzo, invece le scuole progettate in questo programma offriranno due corsi di studio o indirizzi.

Cosi' il liceo linguistico, il liceo classico, gli istituti tecnici agrari e quelli commerciali per esempio offriranno due specializzazioni invece di una. Questo modo di affrontare l'organizzazione delle scuole fornisce agli studenti una grossa opportunita',

Curriculum
In Italy, the curriculum for high schools is organized in specialties or tracks. The precise curriculum for each track is specified in the "Programmi Scolastici Pirola" curriculum guides based on Italian educational laws.

Normally Italian high schools offer one discipline or track. The schools planned in this program will offer two courses of study. That is, instead of the facility supporting just one discipline, e.g. Liceo Linguistico or Liceo Classico or Istituti Tecnici Agrari, the school offers two disciplines. This approach not only provides a greater opportunity for students, it also anticipates

**HONG KONG—
HIGH-RISE HIGH
SCHOOL**

Our firm became involved with developing educational specifications for a new high school building for the Hong Kong International School after the site had been selected. Buildable land is scarce in Hong Kong and the site selected by the Board was a miniscule two-and-a-half-acres situated at the top of a steep slope. To accommodate a full scholastic and recreational program for 720 students in grades 9-12 as well as vehicle parking space obviously required that the school be turned on end and a high-rise facility built. Trying to plan contiguous spaces for compatible functions provided real problems. Where on level sites an integral activity space may be just down the hall, in a high-rise it may have to be upstairs—not exactly contiguous.

Planning Up

We had been recommended as potential educational facility planners by an architect whom we had known years before in Saudi Arabia. The school subsequently sent a representative to Palo Alto and asked our assistance in escorting him around the United States to visit high-rise high schools. Since there are few high-rise schools here and most

Sectioned Elevation, HKIS

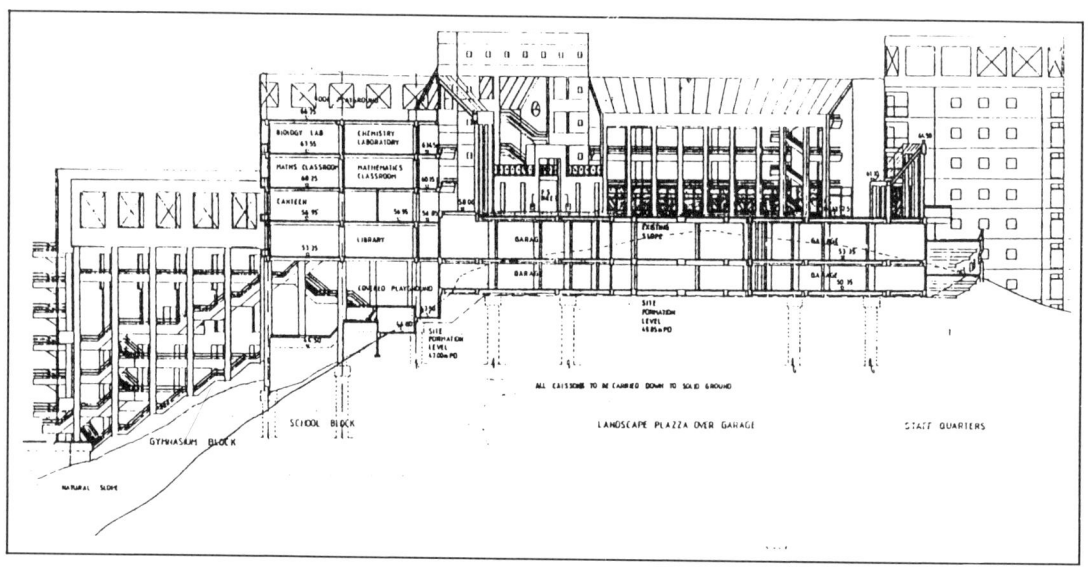

180

of them are less than satisfactory, we persuaded their delegate to spend his time learning about our philosophy of functional planning for schools and touring some problem sites in which solutions based on good planning had resulted. I was subsequently invited to Hong Kong for an interview by the directors of the school.

Although plans were well underway to spend some twelve million U.S. dollars for construction when we first became involved, little attention had been devoted to the educational reason for this sizeable expenditure. No planning had been done as to the present and future nature of the educational experiences the building was to house.

At the board meeting in Hong Kong, after explaining what our company did, I was asked to present a tentative schedule as to the time it would take to do the work as well as the costs. I explained that I was not familiar with the anticipated scope of the project and since this was late November, 1985, we probably would not get much done until the first of January, 1986. However, I would have an estimate by the next day prior to my leaving for the States.

At this point I was interrupted by the president of the Board who informed me that if I wanted the job it would be necessary for me to arrange to have staff on the site by the following Monday and that he wanted the study completed by December 26! Of course we wanted the job. Fortunately I was able to reach my colleague, Howard Sagehorn, who was sitting down to his Thanksgiving dinner. He skipped dessert and flew into Hong Kong and we began interviewing the school staff as a first part of the study by the following Monday—right on the president's schedule.

Like Yesterday!

The complexities of planning that nine-story school on a two-and-a-half-acre site were legion but the Chinese architect, Patrick Lau, provided especially creative designs. This was his first attempt at creating spaces to accommodate educational specifications prepared by specialists from the United

States. We were later engaged to do the specifications for the furniture and equipment for the facility.

While enroute to Bangkok in mid-1987, we had the opportunity to visit the site and witness the hand digging of holes to accommodate the caissons that will support the huge structure. If completed on schedule the school will be ready for occupancy in the fall of 1988.

First Floor Layout, Hong Kong International School

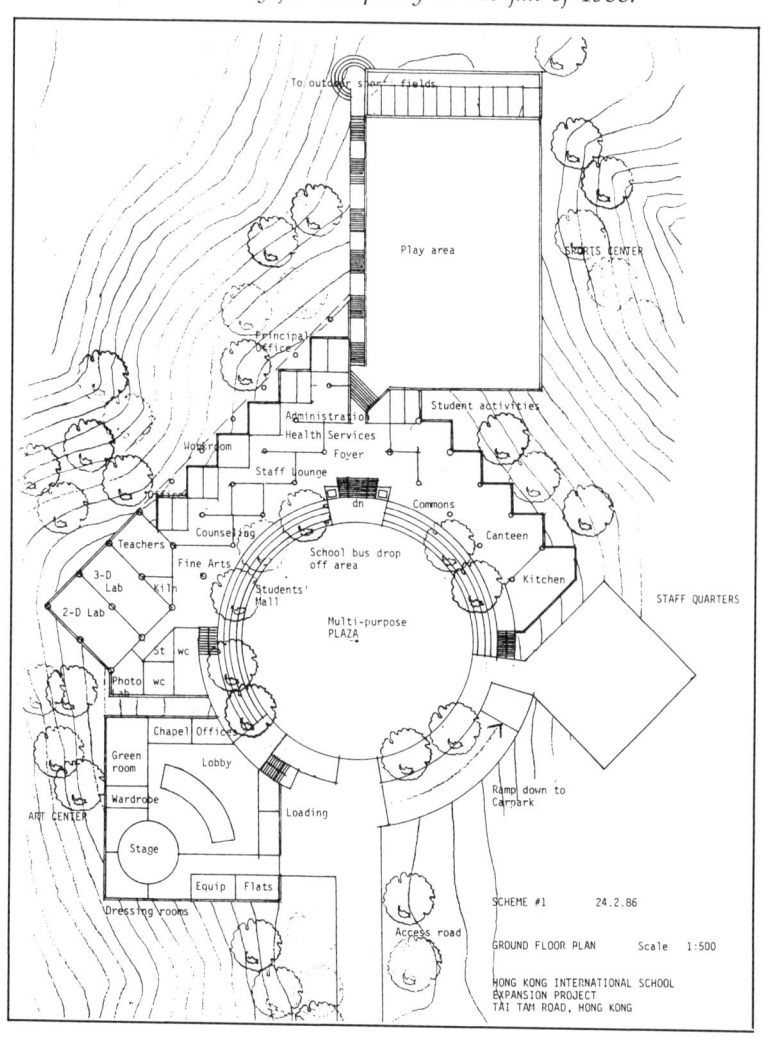

Once a consulting firm has been established, the next task is to locate clients who can use your services, and the next task is to persuade the prospective client that your firm is the one that is the best suited to perform the services needed.

There are a variety of media available to spread the word that your firm is the one that can do the best job. Our experience to date has proven beyond a doubt that word of mouth is still our best device for getting new business. The project for the International School Bangkok in Thailand is an excellent example of that means of advertising.

In May of 1986 I received a telephone call from James Kennedy, a representative of the United States Department of Commerce. He was assisting the school in searching for an educational consulting firm that would be able to help them in a school remodeling program. He had been informed by the administrator of the Hong Kong International School that our firm was doing an excellent job for them. This word-of-mouth contact resulted in our doing one of our larger studies for the International School Bangkok.

THAILAND—INTERNATIONAL SCHOOL BANGKOK

Part of 300 page ISB Report

```
             VI.   PROJECT SUMMARIES

The new ISB School is to be built for grades K-12.  It is to be
occupied in 1990 and ultimately accommodate 2000 students.

The facilities will greatly enhance the current educational program.
In addition to instructional stations there will be a large Media
Center, Fine Arts Center (theater, art and music facility), exten-
sive indoor instructional capabilities, improved PE spaces and a
wide array of support facilities.

These Educational Specifications will enable the architect to under-
stand the school's needs and assist him in developing a design in
keeping with the unique nature of the International School concept.
The consultants understand that there is no one architectural solu-
tion, but that there will be one that is better for ISB than others.
Constant architect and school representative communication is a must.
```

Every study is different and this study was "more different" than most. When I met with the Headmaster and Board in Thailand I was presented with a problem and their suggested solution that to me would not be satisfactory educationally in the long range.

The school was facing growth demands that the existing facility would not accommodate. It was located on an eight-acre site in the midst of a burgeoning business area of the city. Buses on which most of the students arrived created traffic problems in the overcrowded streets. The Board was considering adding a middle school thereby diminishing one of the recreational areas and possibly utilizing an apartment house across the busy street to house part of the school.

Architect's ISB Time Line

ASSIGNMENT TASKS	ESTIMATED ELAPSED WEEKS	February 1987
1. Press announcement - invite developers	1	
2. Prepare developers' brief	1	
3. Prepare Campus Information Profile for Community	1	
4. Brief developers		
5. Short list developers	1	
6. Specify educational requirements : MacConnell	4.5	
7. Prepare design specification and conceptual design	4.5	
8. Receive tenders from developers	8	
9. Prepare Position Statement for AGM	2	
10. Evaluate tenders from developers	4	
11. Prepare educational concept master plan	4	
12. Conduct financial assessment of tenders	4	
13. Preliminary selection of developer(s)	1	
14. Selection of developer	2	
15. Negotiations with developer	2	
16. Prepare Campus Outline Prospectus	2	
17. Architectural designs, calculations and drawings	16	
18. Preparation of three dimensional scale model	2	
19. Complete Campus Prospectus	3	
20. Approval of detailed constructions drawings	2	
21. Obtain necessary permits and licences	6	
22. Construction commences	87	
23. Conduct preliminary financing analyses	4	
24. Detail educational facilities specification	4	
25. Interior designs	12	
26. Investigate financing options	4	
27. Arrange Finance	4	
28. Furnishings and equipment procurement and installation	9	

My suggestion that they were considering the feasibility of installing new pistons in a Model T Ford, and expecting that the automobile would then perform like a Buick, was not met with great enthusiasm.

JDM Passport Renewal, 1988

The upshot of the suggestion, however, was that the Board would consider finding a new school site, out of the traffic congestion, that would provide adequate space to accommodate the facilities for a proposed K-12 school of 2000 students. We were asked to develop the educational specifications that would enable an architect to complete the design for such a new school.

The financial ramifications of moving and building a new plant were substantially in excess of what the original Board solution was. However, the Board appeared equal to the challenge of raising additional funds.

Our specifications have been completed and we are awaiting word as this book goes to press as to whether or not the Board was successful in locating a new site and arranging the financing to facilitate the move.

ON CONSULTING OVERSEAS

Of one thing we are certain about consulting abroad: wherever one works in the educational field, there are differences of opinion as to what the future will bring. You learn that you have to instill confidence in those with whom you are working if you expect your ideas to be considered. You respect the customs and actions of your host colleagues, and constantly remind yourself that this is their country and that you are a visitor. You realize that as Americans, we have a fairly high opinion of our thought processes and solutions, but that these are often totally disregarded as we observe other cultures treating identical problems quite differently, yet coming up with satisfactory solutions.

And In Conclusion

So ends the saga of my first eighty years. For forty of them I have been actively involved in planning *for* schools, hence the title of this book. At press time I was still ensconced in my Palo Alto office with activities divided among daily conferences with colleagues, responding to requests for planning proposals, and reacting to telephone calls urging my participation in great investment opportunities ("Just send cash and be assured of munificient income in your old age.")

Since the book ended abruptly with the report of my last major project, it seems appropriate to add this section by way of a graceful closing. Included are an appreciation for friends, a few stories I have told over the years, and a short epilogue.

AN APPRECIATION FOR MY FRIENDS

If you have searched these pages in vain for your name, don't be alarmed because it isn't here. My original plan was to write something nice about each one of you, but the pages began to mount up and I found myself telling more about my friends than about myself—and after all this is an autobiography and supposed to be about me. So I went to Plan II and thought I would just list the names of all of you people, but still the pages mounted up and I had the fear that I would leave one of you out and you would be upset and take my name off your Chirstmas list.

So I've invoked Plan III which is simply to say "Thank you" from the bottom of my heart to all of you friends, colleagues and family who gave me a boost along the way. You and I can each recall specific events that occurred to cement our friendship and I want you to know that I do appreciate your help. I couldn't have survived these eighty years without you.

SOME CAN TELL 'EM—SOME CAN'T

When learning that I was writing this book several of my colleagues suggested that it would be a good idea to include some of the stories I had accumulated over the years—in fact one went so far as to imply that my autobiographical output might be termed a joke (book).

Be that as it may, telling stories orally and writing them down for others to read and chuckle at is as different as night from day. The environment in which a story is told, the lead-up to the punch line, the sense of timing required are more easily executed in person than from a printed page. You also have the advantage of laughing at your own story. Since laughter is supposed to be contagious, you can encourage your listeners to laugh—whether or not the point of the story is clear to them.

Over the years I have found humor to be a valuable asset. Injected into a tense meeting, an appropriate story often will de-fuse a charged atmosphere and allow normal discussion to proceed. I've learned, however, that the story must not be too subtle as apparently was the case when I was making a presentation to a community in the Northern California hills while trying to get a master planning contract.

A board member asked me what we would do to protect their children from an atomic bomb attack. Instead of explaining to him that underground schools were the only satisfactory protection but that the costs were prohibitive, I jokingly answered that if there were any bombs left for that community the situation would be hopeless anyway. No one laughed and I didn't get the contract.

About Speaking

When on a program with many outstanding speakers I often feel a sense of kinship with William Howard Taft's great granddaughter who wrote in her third grade autobiography: "My great grandfather was President of the United States, my grandfather was a United States Senator, my father was an ambassador, and I am a Brownie."

During lecture tours when the listeners are often too courteous, it is always beneficial to have someone on hand to curb your ego. My wife accompanied me to a PTA talk one evening and afterwards the people stood in line to compliment me on the presentation. A kind lady shook my hand and said, "I think you are one of the great speakers of today." On the way home I asked June, "I wonder how many great speakers there are in this day and age?" To which she answered, "One fewer than you think."

You have to roll with the punches when making presentations, and be able to judge the makeup of the audience. That is why I usually try to arrive early—not only to case the situation, but also to put the chairman of the event at ease by reassuring him or her that the speaker has arrived.

While I was addressing a joint service club meeting about the high quality education being obtained by their children, a father stood up and asked, "If the schools are so good, why can't my fifth grade son read or write?" I knew from talking with a number of the men at the preceding dinner that the schools in that community were well respected. So I took a chance and replied, "It could be 'like father like son.'" The crowd roared and I knew I had guessed right.

Coffee Time

One usually learns the hard way not to answer strange sounding questions after a presentation. While on a speaking tour in Hawaii with some of my Stanford colleagues, a farmer in the audience asked what I thought about the coffee break. I couldn't logically tie my talk on education to a coffee break, but I spent twenty minutes talking about the morale of working groups, the need for management to keep employees happy and so on.

I finally stopped talking—primarily because of the puzzled look on the face of the man who had asked the question. "Professor," he said, "Coffee beans must be picked when they are ripe. It's often six weeks between the times the first and last ones ripen. Our schools are closed during that six week period. We call it the coffee break, and I want to hear you discuss the educational implications of this time that our schools lose each year."

You can imagine what great delight my colleagues took on the remaining days of the tour—leaving a slot on every agenda for MacConnell to expound on "The Coffee Break".

June says it only takes the drop of a hat to get me to talk about the advantages of a well-educated America. She says that when I am lying in my coffin, her last act will be to whisper in my ear, "Someone just called and wants you to make a speech about education." Then if I don't jump up and start for the door, she will turn to the undertaker and say, "Bury him, he's dead for sure!"

During these changing times, it is important to recognize that a situation has changed, or it may be too late to take action as this story illustrates. Tom and Dick were walking down the railroad track discussing world politics and paying little attention to local hazards. When a roar was heard from behind, Tom jumped off the track. After the train passed he found himself alone as he clambered back on the rails. Walking along, he soon came upon a hand, then a foot and finally a head. "My God," he said, "Something must have happened to Dick!"

Changing Times

MacConnell in Action

I guess inflation is here. In 1938 you could buy a Pontiac automobile for $900. In 1988 you can still buy a Pontiac for $900 but if you want the extras like engine and wheels, it will run you $17,000.

On Education

A father, reprimanding his son for always being at the bottom of the class, was informed by the boy that it made little difference, for the same things were taught at both ends.

As a mother sat on the bed and listened to her eight-year-old daughter say her prayers she heard, "And God, make seven times six equal forty-eight." "And why did you say that?" asked her surprised mother. "'Cause that's the way I wrote it on the test today, and I want it to be right."

While visiting a community college I was amused by the initiative displayed by an ingenious student. Under a printed sign reading, "Help Keep this Campus Clean," he had scribbled, "Eat a Pigeon Every Day."

I have always been amazed at how much we expect students to know, and yet become disappointed when incidents come up that prove our inability to extract the correct answer to a question. A teacher in a village school asked her star pupil to stand up and form a sentence containing the word, "seldom." The pupil paused as if in deep thought, and then with enthusiasm replied, "Last week my father had three horses, but yesterday he seldom."

On Traveling

Traveling has its advantages and disadvantages, but on the whole I feel that it has opened many windows for me as well as making me a more understanding person. I learned that to get the most out of traveling, and especially flying on commercial planes, one should take advantage of the many opportunities to converse with others who are also confined to limited quarters for long periods of time.

When planes first began flying from coast to coast, a father took his son on a San Francisco to New York flight and as each of the routine fuel stops were made along the way a red truck would appear to put gas in the plane. Upon arriving in New York, the same fueling activity was again performed. "Son," said the father. "Just think of it!" We have flown all across the United States in less than twelve hours." To which the son replied, "And that little red truck didn't do too badly either."

One morning I was sitting next to an elderly lady on a crowded 747. As the pilot passed her on his way to the cockpit she pulled his coattail and said, "Now please don't fly faster than sound. My friend and I want to talk."

Time zone changes cause interesting interpretations in flight schedules. A young man at the flight counter in Phoenix asked, "What time does the plane leave for Las Vegas?" To which the counter person replied, "7:01 AM." The young man asked the next obvious question, "What time does it get to Las Vegas?" The counter person responded, "7:02 AM. Do you want a ticket?" "No," said the youth. "I just want to go out to the runway and watch it take off."

On Reality

Sometimes people fail to succeed because they misinterpret reality. Two lumberjacks were walking down First Street in Alpena. Neither of them was too well informed on the prominent secret lodges in the city. As they passed by the one-story Independent Order of Odd Fellows Lodge and viewed the traditional "IOOF" logo above the door, one said to the other, "Who would believe that building is 100 feet tall?"

Two men were walking by Saint Patrick's Church in Alpena when the chimes started ringing. "Listen to those beautiful chimes," said one. The other put his hand in back of his ear and said "What?" "Listen to those beautiful chimes," the first man repeated. Again the second put his hand back of his ear and said, "I can't hear a word you're saying because of the racket those damn bells are making!"

Life's Vicissitudes

Having a strong desire to live a healthy life, I try to walk or swim four or five times a week. After each exercise program I think of the two angels who were recently admitted through the pearly gates and were enjoying their newly acquired status in Heaven as they floated from one cloud to another. The first remarked to the other, "Isn't this great," and was reminded by the other one that it was a true statement but had they not participated in that jogging program they could have been enjoying this experience ten years earlier.

A patient was lying with his arms and legs bound and an oxygen hose in his nose. When the priest questioned him about his ability to talk, he received a negative signal from a shake of the man's head, but received a favorable response when asked about his ability to write. The priest handed a slip of paper to the patient who as he was writing, suddenly closed his eyes and apparently passed on to his reward. The priest called a nurse who in turn signaled for a doctor. The doctor confirmed the sudden death but was shocked because he felt that the patient was doing well. While the priest was consoling the widow at the funeral, he reached into his pocket and produced the folded note that he had not read at the deceased's bedside. "I was the last one to have any communications with your husband, and no doubt you will want to save this note," he said to the grieving wife. Together they read the deceased's final message: "You are standing on my air hose!"

Many of us are standing on other people's air hoses as well as our own, and although the consequences are usually not deadly, progress is always impeded.

More Vicissitudes

A husband and wife had not gotten along too well in their long marriage. Finally, to her relief, he passed away. As his body lay in state in the living room, a neighbor lady came in. She placed her hand on that of the deceased, and stated, "Hannah, he is still warm." Whereupon the wife replied, "Warm or cold, he's getting out of here by 10 o'clock this morning!"

Two cats were sitting on a fence during a tennis game. One of them followed the ball closely as it was bounced from one player to the other. The cat who wasn't watching said to the other one, "Why are you so interested in tennis?" To which the first replied, "My old man is in the racket!"

The carving on the tombstone of the hypochondriac read: "I told you all of the time that I was sick."

And In Conclusion

You may be tired of reading these stories. If so remember what I say to my audience when they are getting restless. I remind them of the remark made by the monkey who caught his tail in the lawnmower: "It won't be long now."

I have found in making presentations that it's a good idea to complete the address on a somewhat positive and light note. One of my favorites is, "Now I will say to you what I say to my wife as she leaves for an appointment at the beauty parlor—Good Luck."

EPILOGUE

I don't expect any great events to occur because I have shared part of my life story with you. However, it does provide a little history of a farm boy in somewhat straitened circumstances who wanted to get ahead. Because he did so it might encourage a few young people who when faced with similar conditions may be inclined to give up.

Doors of opportunity are open to most of us on occasion—sometimes wide open and sometimes barely ajar—but open. If we set goals for ourselves and make the preparations necessary to achieve the goals and develop tenacity of spirit, we will be in a position to recognize and take advantage of the doors of opportunity whenever they open for us.

Remember the story of the two frogs who fell into a crock of cream one night? One gave up and drowned while the other one started to swim and when daylight came found himself sitting on a patty of butter.

I asked a best-selling author what his formula for success was. He responded that he tries to tailor his writing as if he were designing a woman's nightgown. He makes it long enough to cover the subject but short enough to make it interesting. I realize that I shall never be known as a successful nightgown designer or author, but I do hope that what you read here was interesting and not too long.